Prayers

OF THE PEOPLE

Patterns and Models for Congregational Prayer

Second Edition

FROM THE *Worship* SOURCEBOOK

CALVIN INSTITUTE OF
CHRISTIAN WORSHIP
for the study and renewal of worship

FAITH
ALIVE.
Christian Resources

Prayers of the People: Patterns and Models for Congregational Prayer

Copublished by

The Calvin Institute of Christian Worship, 1855 Knollcrest Circle SE, Grand Rapids, MI 49546-4402; phone: (616) 526-6088; e-mail: worship@calvin.edu; website: www.calvin.edu/worship.

Faith Alive Christian Resources, 1700 28th St. SE, Grand Rapids, MI 49508; phone: (800) 333-8300; website: www.FaithAliveResources.org.

For the use of numerous Scripture and other texts printed in this book the publisher gratefully acknowledges permissions granted by copyright holders as referenced in Acknowledgments, which hereby becomes an extension of this copyright page.

Printed in the United States of America on recycled paper.

Library of Congress Cataloging-in-Publication Data
Prayers of the people: patterns and models for congregational prayer.
     p.   cm.
   Includes index.
   ISBN 978-1-59255-680-9
   1. Prayer—Christianity. 2. Public worship. I. CRC Publications (Grand Rapids, Mich.) II. Calvin Institute of Christian Worship. III. Worship sourcebook. IV. Title.
   BV226.P69   2004
   264'.1—dc22

                                                            2004014482

10 9 8 7 6 5 4 3 2 1

TABLE OF CONTENTS

PREFACE

A typical worship service includes many prayers, such as an opening prayer of adoration and praise, a prayer of confession, a prayer for illumination before the Scripture reading and sermon, and a prayer after the sermon. These prayers are usually spoken by a pastor or another worship leader. In addition, many songs are prayers, sung by all worship participants.

One type of prayer stands apart, however, as the church offers thanksgiving and intercedes for local, national, and global communities. This prayer is usually the longest and most inclusive prayer of the service. Known in some traditions as the "congregational prayer," it's also one of the most challenging to prepare in such a way that, while led by one or just a few people, it becomes the prayer of all the worshipers, the "prayers of the people."

As growing numbers of churches use the gifts of various members to lead in such congregational prayer, this little book, *Prayers of the People,* aims to offer guidance and models for leading this kind of prayer. The contents of this book are from *The Worship Sourcebook,* a larger collection of resources for use in all parts of the worship service. Since that larger collection is used mainly by pastors and worship planners, this smaller collection is available to make the "prayers of the people" from *The Worship Sourcebook* more easily accessible to the wider group of people who participate in leading congregational prayer.

We dedicate *Prayers of the People* to the hundreds of faithful pastors, worship planners, prayer leaders, and wordsmiths who work each week, often with remarkable generosity, creativity, and resourcefulness, to prepare and lead God-glorifying worship in congregations everywhere.

Emily R. Brink, former editor, *Reformed Worship*
John D. Witvliet, director, Calvin Institute of
Christian Worship

INTRODUCTION

Intercessory Prayer, the Prayers of the People

One of the central acts of worship is the intercessory prayer. In some churches this is known as the "pastoral prayer," but "congregational prayer" or "prayers of the people" is preferable. This prayer is spoken on behalf of the entire congregation. Calling it the intercessory prayer is also helpful, of course, since that name calls attention to the prayer's primary purpose.

In the intercessory prayer we address God in a special way as priestly intercessors for each other and for the world at large. We pray not just for our own congregation and for the people we know; we also intercede for those in authority, for those suffering oppression, for those who are poor, hungry, or sick, and so on. If this is the only prayer offered during a worship service, it can also appropriately include adoration, confession, and thanksgiving as well as intercession. If those elements are present in other parts of the service, however, then it will usually be fitting for the prayers of the people to focus mainly on intercession.

The intercessory prayer may include not only words but also periods of silence and sung prayers, such as a refrain or a stanza of a hymn. Prayers may be offered while standing with arms raised (see Ps. 141), kneeling, or seated with hands folded and head bowed. Prayers may be offered from the pulpit, from the communion table, from the baptismal font, or from among the congregation.

Sometimes the pastor or another member of the congregation offers a prayer on behalf of the congregation. At other times everyone prays in unison, or the congregation and leader pray by following a litany. The intercessory prayer may be offered in various ways by a variety of worshipers gathered. Some older members, officebearers, and young people may be able to lead the congregation in prayer. Some may be gifted in writing their own prayers. Others may be able to read well, making a prayer written by someone else come alive.

Christian congregations have produced many models, patterns, and habits for structuring prayer. The best of models feature both disciplined balance (to address a variety of concerns over time) and flexibility (to express the unique circumstances of a given moment). The model most suitable for a congregation's regular worship services will depend mainly on the size of the congregation, the degree of participation that can be achieved, and the expectations of the congregation.

Note that all the prayers presented in this book end with "Amen" in boldface. The purpose of the "Amen" (which means "this is sure to be") is to invite worshipers to add their voice of assent to the prayer, reinforcing the understanding that the prayer is offered by everyone. Sometimes worship leaders invite the congregation to voice the "Amen" by ending their prayer with the words "And all God's people say . . ." Others might encourage their congregation to spontaneously say "Amen" at the end of every prayer.

The Language of Prayer

"I often think of the set pieces of liturgy as certain words which people have successfully addressed to God without their getting killed."

—Annie Dillard

Worship is much more than words, of course. And often prayers feature too many words. We may long for worship that breathes with silence and meditation or for instrumental music that transcends words. Still, worship depends on words. God's revelation to us is given not only in creation but also in words that communicate all we need to know about God, ourselves, and our salvation. Our communal worship is made possible because we have words to speak to each other, to call each other to worship, to speak common prayers, and to encourage each other in the faith.

Yet the words of our worship often don't get the attention that our music does. We often devote hundreds of rehearsal hours to music each year, but very few to selecting how we will speak to God in worship. Yet language, like music, is an art to be received and cultivated as a gift from God. Liturgical cliché is not a virtue. As art, language can be immeasurably enhanced by creativity, imagination, and forethought—all of which need not preclude the energy and immediacy of extemporaneous prayer.

Perhaps the largest challenge for the language of worship is that one set of words—usually spoken or prepared by a single person—needs to somehow embrace, express, and elicit the worship of a whole group of people. From the perspective of a worshiper, *public* worship always involves using words that come from someone else. One skill for worshipers to hone is the skill of "learning to mean the words that someone else gives us," whether those are the words of a songwriter or prayer leader. This skill requires a unique mix of humility (submitting ourselves to words given to us by the community of faith), grace (willingness to offer the benefit of the doubt when those words may not have been well chosen), and intention (to actually appropriate those words as our own).

Certainly the ideal is a worship service in which each worshiper in the community is unself-consciously engaged with heart, mind, soul, and will and really means every good word that is spoken or sung. Yet not everyone who sings songs of praise has heart, mind, and will engaged every moment. Not all who speak the Lord's Prayer, for example, are "meaning it" at the moment. And although worshipers' later reports or body language can give us some clues about whether they are meaning it, we never know this with certainty. Some who appear less engaged may actually be deeply engaged. Others who are vigorously participating may be more caught up with the music or beauty of the language than the act of worship itself. The goal for language in worship, as it is for music, is to do everything possible to elicit and express the community's worship in ways that don't unnecessarily get in the way. This is a goal that is never perfectly attainable. But it is also a practice that can be deepened over time. That deepening happens in part through a use of good models. It also is encouraged by reflecting on the goals and criteria of our language. Consider the following goals and criteria for language in worship.

1. **We need words that are faithful to the content of Scripture and the gospel of Christ.** Many prayers in this book are directly from or are based on Scripture. With this feature we hope to encourage the use of scriptural language in worship. Scriptural texts in this book are from a variety of Bible versions and are referenced as exact quotations, as slight adaptations (noted as "from" a particular text), or as paraphrases or quotations coupled with additional phrasing (noted as "based on" a particular text). Some other resources also include references to Scripture texts; an index of Scripture references (p. 85) offers additional Scripture source information as an aid to worship planning.

2. **We need words that offer a balanced diet of biblical themes.** We need to speak of God as both a mighty sovereign and a tender encourager. We need to speak of Jesus Christ as both Savior and Lord. We need to reflect a balanced piety that stresses that salvation in Christ is intensely personal but that it also extends to creation and culture. We need to speak of the church, the community of believers, as a community called to embrace truth and to extend hospitality, to witness to the gospel of Christ and to work for justice and peace on earth.

    Language about God has been especially contentious in our time. This volume reflects a commitment to focus in on and to draw more intentionally on the wide range of names, metaphors, and images used explicitly in Scripture to shape our language about God. This approach will not satisfy everyone, but we pray that this book will provide a helpful point of departure, especially for congregations having conflicts over language issues.

3. **We need words that members of the congregation can appropriate as their own.** The language of prayer should be both accessible and reverent, both understandable and evocative. The language of worship should enable the participation of all members of the body, young and old, brand-new Christians and lifelong believers alike. Many prayers in litany form, for example, encourage congregational participation (as noted by bold print), sometimes also calling for additional responsive use. Leaders may alter boldfacing as they wish to suit the needs and style of their congregation's participation. Most churches need to work to expand worshipers' participation in corporate prayer. Patterns of participation cannot be mastered in one service. They must become habits—in the best sense.

4. **We need words that both express our experience and form us for a deeper experience.** A healthy prayer life, both private and public, involves two kinds of prayers. First, some prayers are specific, extemporaneous, personal, and immediate. These prayers arise from the honesty of our own experience—for example, "Lord God, help our congregation in this time of great uncertainty and even fear. . . ." Second, some prayers are communal or "given," even "imposed" on us. Think of children learning the Lord's Prayer. They may learn this prayer before they even understand the words, but they grow into it over time, learning to pray it more and more sincerely throughout their entire lives. Think also of an evangelist's invitation: "Pray this prayer with me." Or the practice of praying the Psalms. In all these examples, we can be grateful that our prayer life is not limited to what we can generate from our own thoughts, experiences, and emotions but that we are invited to grow into something bigger than ourselves.

5. **Worship at its best features a balance of extemporaneous and prepared prayers.** In other words, just because this book contains prepared prayers does not imply that every worship service should feature only prewritten prayers. The goal is not to impose uniformity on worship but rather to provide reliable, trustworthy resources, drawing on the riches of the Christian tradition to help leaders be good stewards of the words they use in worship. We should also remember that most songs are prepared prayers; the challenge is to pray as we sing.

6. **Worship at its best is intergenerational.** Worship leaders need to invite children to be full, conscious, active participants, not just onlookers. The potential for children's participation varies greatly from congregation to congregation, depending on the nature and level of biblical literacy and education programs. Children are able to participate in worship much more

fully than many churches encourage or allow. For that to happen, the language of prayer should be appropriately accessible. Leaders may well need to adapt some texts so that the tone, rhetoric, and content are appropriate for all participants.

7. **Worship at its best is prepared in advance.** Some leaders may have every word printed out, others may lead from a prepared outline, and still others may speak entirely extemporaneously. But even if you lead extemporaneously, consider preparing to lead in prayer (or other aspects of worship) by writing your prayers out before leaving the script behind. Extemporaneous or spontaneous prayers often leave us to rely on all-too-familiar phrases and expressions. For example, we might pray, "Be with our missionaries. Be with our friends. Be with our families." Writing a prayer out or adapting another resource forces us to think about our language and to avoid language that becomes monotonous or even meaningless through overuse. Even if you leave your script behind and offer the prayer without notes, a journaling or adaptation exercise will challenge you to use fresh language and consider the balance and vitality of your language.

One final note about the words we use in worship and the words contained in this book: words in a book are no more useful than musical notes on a page. Their effectiveness depends on how the words are brought to life through speech. The same prayer, read from a manuscript, book, or bulletin, can be either lifeless or life giving. It all depends on how the words are actually spoken.

Organization of Resources

This book provides prayer resources for regular Sunday use, along with teaching notes about the meaning and use of various types of prayers included within. All of these resources are from Section 4: Prayers of the People of *The Worship Sourcebook.*

For ease of reference, each section is assigned a number, and each resource within each section is also numbered. All that's needed to identify a resource, then, is to cite the section number and resource number.

For example, resource 1.5, an invitation to prayer, is found in section 1 (Invitations to Prayer) under resource number 5 ("Let us join in prayer . . .").

For easy identification of Scripture and confessional texts in this book, we've included credit lines immediately following those particular texts. You may also wish to identify the sources of other items; we did not place credits next to those items, preferring that they be presented without the distraction of numerous and sometimes lengthy credit lines. However, there are appropriate occasions for including that information as well. To identify sources, you can look up their respective resource numbers (for example, 1.5 or 4.25) in the Acknowledgments section, which supplies all necessary source information for resources used in this book. In addition, if you are looking for a prayer from a particular author or collection, you can find the author's name or collection title in the Acknowledgments section.

For each resource used in a printed bulletin or on a projection system, we ask that you include the following acknowledgment: "Reprinted by permission from *Prayers of the People: Patterns and Models for Congregational Prayer*, © 2015, Faith Alive Christian Resources." This notice can appear in small print preferably on the same page on which the resource is reprinted. To keep records, you'll want to record the resource number (such as 1.4 or 4.25) on your worship planning documents and write the date used next to the text in this book.

As much as you are able, use this resource book to God's honor and glory!

John D. Witvliet, director, Calvin Institute of
Christian Worship

PRAYERS OF THE PEOPLE

1 INVITATIONS TO PRAYER

The following simple introductions to prayer emphasize the corporate nature of prayer. They stand in contrast to the familiar phrase "Please join me in prayer," which can imply that the prayer is an individual prayer of the leader to which others are invited to listen.

1   We offer now our prayers of thanksgiving and intercession.

2   We join our hearts and voices to offer our prayers to God.

3   We pray together now in Jesus' name.

4   We offer our prayers together now, uniting our voices with Christ, who perfects our prayers.

5   Let us join in prayer, offering our praise, thanksgiving, and intercession to God.

6   Let us bring our thanksgiving and concerns before God in prayer.

7   Let us pray for the growth of God's kingdom in our world today.

8   God calls us to be a praying people.
    Let us join in prayer, offering our praise, thanksgiving, and intercession to God.

Intercessory prayer is a matter of Christian obedience. We pray in response to God's invitation and command. The following texts convey both the privilege and significance of prayer. After each of the following texts, add a phrase of introduction from numbers 1-8 above.

9   Our help is in the name of the LORD,
    who made heaven and earth.
        —Psalm 124:8, NRSV

10   Let all who are faithful
     offer prayer to you;
     at a time of distress,
     the rush of mighty waters shall not reach them.
          —Psalm 32:6, NRSV

11   The Spirit helps us in our weakness;
     for we do not know how to pray as we ought,
     but that very Spirit intercedes with sighs too deep for words.
     And God, who searches the heart,
     knows what is the mind of the Spirit,
     because the Spirit intercedes for the saints according to the will of God.
          —Romans 8:26-27, NRSV

12   Pray in the Spirit at all times
     in every prayer and supplication.
     To that end keep alert and always persevere
     in supplication for all the saints.
          —Ephesians 6:18, NRSV

13   Do not worry about anything,
     but in everything by prayer and supplication
     with thanksgiving let your requests be made known to God.
     And the peace of God, which surpasses all understanding,
     will guard your hearts and your minds in Christ Jesus.
          —Philippians 4:6-7, NRSV

14   First of all, then, I urge that supplications, prayers,
     intercessions, and thanksgivings be made for everyone,
     for kings and all who are in high positions,
     so that we may lead a quiet and peaceable life
     in all godliness and dignity.
     This is right and is acceptable in the sight of God our Savior,
     who desires everyone to be saved
     and to come to the knowledge of the truth.
          —1 Timothy 2:1-4, NRSV

15   As Christians, we believe that
     prayer is the most important part
     of the thankfulness God requires of us.
     We also believe that God gives his grace and Holy Spirit
     only to those who pray continually and groan inwardly,
     asking God for these gifts
     and thanking him for them.
          —from Heidelberg Catechism, Q&A 116

16   The prayer our Savior taught us begins with the words
"Our Father in heaven."
With this address, Christ aims to stir
in our hearts a childlike awe and trust
because through Christ God has become our Father.
God, our Father, loves us and desires what is best for us.
God, our Father, answers our prayers.
So let us come with reverence and confidence,
trusting in our Father's mercies through Jesus Christ.
—based on Heidelberg Catechism, Q&A 120

17   God is the one who makes us, loves us, and sustains us.
God is the one who makes, loves, and sustains the world.

18   Nothing in all creation can separate us from God's love;
we put all our experiences, all our lives, in God's hands.

2 GATHERING PRAYER REQUESTS

To live up to its name, the "prayers of the people" should express a broad range of both thanksgiving and petition that reflects the diversity of experience within the congregation. This prayer should also be specific and immediate, expressing the unique circumstances of a congregation at a given time and place. Prayer requests may be gathered in writing prior to a worship service; gathered through a discussion with congregational leaders, worship planners, or a representative group of congregation members; or gathered extemporaneously during the service itself.

At times, lists of prayer concerns can become too narrow or self-centered. The following prompting questions can help expand the range of prayer topics suggested by members of the congregation. Leaders may choose to use a representative sample of these or similar questions each time requests are gathered.

Praise and Thanksgiving

- For which divine actions or attributes shall we bless God?
- For which blessings shall we thank God?
- For which aspects of biblical teaching shall we thank God?

Petitions

- For which country (or part of the world) shall we pray?
- For which ministry shall we pray?

- For which other congregations shall we pray?
- For which aspects of congregational life shall we pray?
- For which concerns in our town or city shall we pray?
- For which personal concerns shall we pray?
- For which voiceless and powerless persons shall we pray?
- For which spiritual gifts shall we pray?

See also "Bidding Prayers" (in section 4.4), which invite worshipers to name specific topics as part of the prayer itself.

3 PREPARING EXTEMPORANEOUS PRAYERS

Extemporaneous prayer is a cherished part of worship in many Christian traditions. It allows for the specific circumstances of the community to be named in both thanksgiving and petition and for the emotions of the community to shape the language of prayer. But extemporaneous prayer can become predictable and cliché-ridden over time—just as can the use of set or written prayers. The following resources offer guidance in preparing extemporaneous prayers to help keep the language of such prayers fresh and thoughtful. With this material, prayer leaders can prepare an outline from which they can pray extemporaneously. These resources cover each main part of prayer: addressing God, praising and thanking God, offering petitions and intercessions, and closing (for prayers of confession, see section 2.2).

Scriptural Names for Addressing God

The following scriptural names for God are provided to help leaders preparing to address God in prayer. At its best, a congregation's prayers address God with a full range of biblical imagery that at once grounds our language about God in Scripture and expands our use of language for God beyond our normal patterns of speech. Often the following names are combined in various ways, such as "Almighty, everlasting God" or "Holy God, our provider."

Names of Address for God

Alpha and Omega
(Rev. 1:8; 22:13)

Almighty and loving God
(Gen. 1:1; Ps. 68:1-6)

Almighty God, giver of strength
(Gen. 17:1; Ex. 6:3-8; Ps. 68:4-14)

Creator
(Isa. 43:15; Rom. 1:25; 1 Pet. 4:19)

Everlasting God
(Gen. 21:33; Isa. 40:28)

Faithful God
(Deut. 7:9; 32:4; Ps. 31:5)

Father of compassion and God of all comfort
(2 Cor. 1:3)

Father of mercies
(2 Cor. 1:3)

God, our healer
(Ex. 15:26)

God, our provider
(Gen. 22:14)

God, our peace, *or* **God of peace**
(Judges 6:24; Heb. 13:20)

God, our purifier
(Ex. 31:13; Lev. 20:8)

God, our righteousness
(Jer. 23:6)

God, our shepherd
(Gen. 49:24; Ps. 23:1; 80:1)

God and Father of Jesus Christ
(Rom. 15:6)

Gracious God
(Jon. 4:2)

Holy God
(Lev. 19:2; Josh. 24:19; Isa. 5:16)

Living God
(Jer. 10:10; 2 Cor. 3:3; 6:16)

Lord
(Gen. 15:2; Ex. 3:14-15; Acts 3:22)

Lord God
(Ps. 68:32; Dan. 9:3)

Lord of hosts
(Josh. 5:14; 1 Sam. 1:3; Ps. 24:10)

Most High God
(Gen. 14:18; Ps. 9:2)

Our Father
(Isa. 64:8; Matt. 6:9; Eph. 1:2)

Redeemer, covenant God
(Ex. 3:14-15; Isa. 49:26)

Refuge
(Ps. 28:8; 46:1; 91:2)

Rock
(2 Sam. 23:3; Hab. 1:12; 1 Cor. 10:4)

Triune God
(derived from 2 Cor. 13:13 and other passages)

Throughout the history of the Christian church, the primary pattern of praying has been "through Jesus Christ in the Spirit" or "in the name of Jesus in the power of the Holy Spirit," a pattern of address that highlights Jesus' role as mediator and the Spirit's work of prompting and empowering prayer. A secondary pattern of prayer has been to address Jesus or the Holy Spirit directly, a practice based on the theological assertion that Jesus Christ and the Holy Spirit are fully divine persons. The following lists provide a sampling of many possible scriptural names and images for addressing Jesus and the Holy Spirit in prayer.

Names of Address for Jesus

Jesus
(Matt. 1:21)

Christ
(Matt. 1:16; 2:4)

Any of the following names or titles may be added, such as "Jesus Christ, our bread of life."

Anointed One
(Ps. 2:2)

Bread of life
(John 6:35)

Bright morning star
(Rev. 22:16)

Cornerstone
(Eph. 2:20; 1 Pet. 2:6-7)

Desire of nations
(Hag. 2:7)

Deliverer
(Rom. 11:26)

Emmanuel
(Matt. 1:23)

Friend of sinners
(Matt. 11:19)

Good shepherd
(John 10:11, 14)

Head of the church
(Col. 1:18)

High Priest
(Heb. 3:1; 4:14)

Holy One of Israel
(Isa. 41:14)

King of kings
(1 Tim. 6:15; Rev. 19:16)

Lamb of God
(John 1:29; 1 Cor. 5:7; Rev. 5:6)

Light of the world
(John 9:5)

Lord of lords
(1 Tim. 6:15; Rev. 19:16)

Master
(Luke 5:5)

Mediator
(1 Tim. 2:5; Heb. 12:24)

Messiah
(John 1:41)

One and Only Son
(John 1:18; 3:16)

Physician
(Matt. 9:12)

Redeemer
(Job 19:25; Isa. 59:20; 60:16)

Savior
(Luke 1:47; 2:11; Titus 3:6)

Servant of God
(Isa. 42:1; 49:5-7)

Son of David
(Matt. 9:27; 15:22)

Son of God
(Matt. 26:63; Luke 1:35)

Son of Man
(Mark 2:10; John 1:51)

Sun of righteousness
(Mal. 4:2)

Teacher
(Mark 10:35; John 20:16)

Wonderful Counselor
(Isa. 9:6)

Way of life
(John 14:6)

Word of God
(John 1:1; Rev. 19:13)

Names of Address for the Holy Spirit

Advocate
(John 14:16, 26)

Breath of God
(Job 32:8; 33:4; John 20:22)

Comforter
(Acts 9:31; 2 Cor. 1:3-7)

Counselor
(John 14:16, 26)

Creator Spirit
(from Gen. 1:2)

Eternal Spirit
(Heb. 9:14)

Holy Spirit
(Isa. 63:10-11; Luke 3:16;
1 Thess. 4:8)

Spirit of adoption
(Rom. 8:15; Gal. 4:4-7)

Spirit of Christ
(Rom. 8:9; 1 Pet. 1:11)

Spirit of God
(Matt. 3:16; Rom. 8:9; Phil. 3.3)

Spirit of holiness
(Rom. 1:4)

Spirit of truth
(John 15:26; 16:13)

Spirit of wisdom
(Isa. 11:2)

Actions and Attributes of God

The following lists cite actions and attributes for which we praise and thank God in prayer. We ground our petitions in God's character by naming particular attributes and actions of God and praising God for them.

The following actions or attributes can be included briefly in a form of address to God (such as "Almighty God, you have given us the gift of the Holy Spirit to lead us to Christ") or in an extended prayer of thanksgiving. These lists merely offer suggestions on the many actions and attributes of God we can refer to in prayer.

17

Actions

Gracious God,
you created the world in beauty . . .
you created us in your image and yet more wonderfully restored us
    in Christ . . .
you are re-creating the world in Christ . . .
you revealed yourself to us in Christ . . .
you allow us to glimpse your glory in the face of Christ . . .
you teach, comfort, and challenge us by your Word . . .
you govern this world in power and love . . .
you lead us faithfully . . .
you led your people by fire and cloud . . .
you prepared the way for the coming of your Son . . .
you sent your Son to the world for its salvation . . .
you led the Magi by a star to worship your Son . . .
you anointed Jesus your Son with your Spirit at his baptism . . .
you raised Jesus from the dead through the power of the Spirit . . .
you send us out into the world to make disciples . . .
you sent your Holy Spirit to point us to Christ . . .
you send your Holy Spirit to empower the church . . .
you hear our prayers in Jesus' name . . .
you promise always to be with us . . .
you promise the coming of Christ's kingdom . . .
you alone can bring healing . . .
you alone can bring unity out of dissension . . .
you alone can conquer evil . . .

Attributes

Gracious God, we praise you as the one who is . . .

abundant in truth	good	just
almighty	gracious	living
beautiful	holy	long-suffering
eternal *or* everlasting	incomprehensible	loving
ever present	infinite	perfect
faithful	invisible	wise

*For extended expressions of praise, each attribute may be linked with a particular text, a narrative
of God's actions in history, or an experience (such as "Gracious Lord, we praise you as the one who
was faithful to Abraham and Sarah, Boaz and Ruth, Joseph and Mary, and even to us . . .").*

*Each of these attributes is complementary. Consider pairing attributes that we might otherwise
think of as opposites (for example, "We praise you, Lord God, as the one whose justice is expressed
in love, and whose love is expressed in justice . . .").*

Scriptural Openings of Prayer

Scripture includes many prayers offered by God's people. While these prayers don't speak of specific contemporary needs or concerns, they provide beautiful and faithful language for addressing God. One way to draw from this language is to use a short, responsive verse of Scripture at the beginning of an intercessory prayer.

1   We pray to you, O Lord;
     you hear our voice in the morning;
     at sunrise we offer our prayers
     and wait for your answer.
           —based on Psalm 5:2-3

2   **May the words of our mouths**
              and the meditations of our hearts,
          be acceptable in your sight,
     O LORD, our Rock and our Redeemer.
           —from Psalm 19:14, NIV

3   To you, O LORD, I lift my soul.
     O God, in you I trust.
           —from Psalm 25:1-2, NRSV

4   Our prayer is to you, O LORD.
         At an acceptable time, O God,
         in the abundance of your steadfast love, answer us.
           —from Psalm 69:13, NRSV

5   O God, come to our assistance.
     O Lord, hasten to help us.
           —based on Psalm 70:1

6   Hear our prayer, O LORD;
     let our cry come to you.
           —from Psalm 102:1, NRSV

7   Let my prayer be counted as incense before you,
     and the lifting up of my hands as an evening sacrifice.
           —Psalm 141:2, NRSV

8   Hear my prayer, O LORD;
         give ear to my supplications in your faithfulness;
         answer me in your righteousness.
           —Psalm 143:1, NRSV

Topics for Petitions

The following list of topics challenges prayer leaders to think of concerns that should be included regularly in public prayer but may be forgotten in light of a given leader's or congregation's experience. This list can serve well as a checklist over time to ensure that a balanced range of concerns is incorporated in a congregation's prayers.

For the Creation

    Harvest
    Environmental concerns
    Natural disasters
    Seasonable weather
    Restoration

For the World

    War
    Injustice
    Hunger
    Disease
    Racial strife
    World governments
    International crisis
    International relief organizations

For the Nation

    Courts and judges
    National leaders
    Upcoming elections
    Military personnel
    Lobbyists and advocates for justice and peace

For the Local Community

    Local government
    Housing
    Racial strife
    Poverty
    Employment
    Government services
    Schools

For the Worldwide Church

    Unity of the church
    Holiness of the church
    Missionaries and mission agencies
    Christian education: schools, colleges, seminaries
    Denominations

Denominational missions and programs
Other Christian traditions

For the Local Church

Pastor(s)
Elders and other leaders
Deacons and others who serve
Staff members
Teachers
Stewards of church finances
Musicians and artists
People leaving for service opportunities
Missionaries
All members in their witness in the community
Thanksgiving for faithful service
Local mission
Congregational anniversary
New or remodeled church building
Unity in the congregation

For Those with Special Needs

Those who suffer with physical illness, and those who care for them
Those who suffer with mental illness, and those who care for them
Those who have intellectual, emotional, and/or behavioral impairments,
    and those who care for them
Those who are elderly and infirm, and those who care for them
Those who have suffered abuse, and those who support them
Those who suffer with addiction, and those who support them
Those who mourn a death, and those who minister to them
Those who are imprisoned, and those who minister to them
Those who are lonely, and those who support them
Those who are orphaned, and those who care for them
Those who are homeless, and those who care for them
Those who are victims of crime, and those who support them
Those whose needs cannot be spoken
Those who are facing temptations

Those who live as single persons
Those who are about to be married or who are newly married
Those who celebrate a wedding anniversary
Those who struggle with marital difficulties
Those who are divorced and separated
Those whose sexuality is a source of pain

Those who celebrate the birth of a child
Those who long for children
Those who adopt a child or children
Those who are adopted

Those who care for young children
Those who care for elderly or needy parents

Those who are just starting school
Those who are struggling with peer pressure
Those who are trying to choose a college or career path
Those who are leaving home

Those who are unemployed or underemployed
Those who work in business and industry
Those who work in homemaking
Those who work in medicine
Those who work in education
Those who work in agriculture
Those who work in government
Those who work in service to others
Those who are beginning a new career
Those who struggle in their work
Those who are seeking new or different jobs
Those who are retired or anticipating retirement

Those who celebrate baptism
Those who celebrate a renewed faith commitment or profession of faith
Those who struggle with doubts
Those who are persecuted for their faith
Those who seek spiritual renewal
Those with family members and friends who do not have faith

Those who travel
Those who are enjoying leisure or rest
Those who traveled to be present at worship

Those who are new members of the congregation
Those who are departing members of the congregation

Prayer Refrains

The following refrains may be used repeatedly throughout an intercessory prayer. Whether the prayer itself is extemporaneous or written out, these refrains enable the congregation to participate by affirming the petitions spoken by the leader.

9   Lord, in your mercy,
     hear our prayer.

10   Let us pray to the Lord.
     Lord, have mercy.

11   Gracious God, hear our prayer.
     And in your love answer.

12 For your love and goodness,
we give you thanks, O God.

13 God of grace, [*or*] God of all mercies,
hear our prayer.

14 Heavenly Father,
hear us as we pray.

15 O God, hear our prayer,
and let our cry come to you.

16 Holy Spirit, our Comforter,
receive our prayer.

17 Holy Spirit,
act through us, we pray.

18 Healing Spirit,
receive our prayer.

19 Give thanks to the LORD, for he is good.
His love endures forever.
—Psalm 136:1, NIV

Concluding Phrases and Prayers

The closing words of prayer help us to pull back from focusing on our concerns and petitions to survey the large spiritual context in which we pray. Common themes include the mediation of Christ (our prayers are in Jesus' name), the glory of God, the wondrous mystery of the Trinity, and our union in Christ with God's people in all times and all places. The close of the prayer may also be a kind of poetic summary of the grand themes of grace and gratitude in the Christian life.

Phrases That Emphasize the Mediating Work of Christ

20 Through Jesus Christ, our Lord. **Amen.**

21 In Jesus' name. **Amen.**

22 In the strong name of Jesus Christ, our Savior. **Amen.**

23 In the name of Jesus Christ,
who lives and reigns with you and the Spirit,
one God, now and forever. **Amen.**

Ascriptions of Praise

24 Yours is the kingdom, the power, and the glory,
now and forever. **Amen.**

25 To you be the glory, now and forever. **Amen.**

26 To your holy name,
with the church on earth and the church in heaven,
we ascribe all honor and glory,
now and forever. **Amen.**

Concluding Prayers That Emphasize Our Union with Believers in All Times and Places

27 Loving God,
we offer these prayers,
joining our voices to the great chorus of those
who sing your praise and depend on you alone.
We long for that day when all your children
will live in your peace and praise your name.
Until that day, give us sturdy patience and enduring hope,
rooted only in Jesus, in whose name we pray. **Amen.**

28 Ever-faithful God,
you have knit together as one body in Christ
those who have been your people in all times and places.
Keep us in communion with all your saints,
following their example of faith and life,
until that day when all your saints will dwell together
in the joy of your eternal kingdom.
Through Christ, our Lord. **Amen.**

Summary Prayers

29 Almighty God, Father of all mercies,
we, your unworthy servants, give you humble thanks
for all your goodness and loving-kindness
to us and to all whom you have made.
**We bless you for our creation, preservation,
and all the blessings of this life,
but above all for your immeasurable love
in the redemption of the world by our Lord Jesus Christ,
for the means of grace, and for the hope of glory.
And, we pray, give us such an awareness of your mercies
that with truly thankful hearts we may show forth your praise,
not only with our lips, but in our lives,
by giving up ourselves to your service,
and by walking before you
in holiness and righteousness all our days,
through Jesus Christ, our Lord,
to whom, with you and the Holy Spirit,
be honor and glory throughout all ages. Amen.**

30 Almighty God,
you have given us grace at this time with one accord
to make our common supplication to you,
and you have promised through your well-beloved Son
that when two or three are gathered together in his name
you will be in the midst of them.
**Fulfill now, O Lord, our desires and petitions
as may be best for us,
granting us in this world knowledge of your truth,
and in the age to come life everlasting. Amen.**

31 Gracious God,
accept all these prayers offered in Jesus' name,
and give us now the strength to wait patiently for your answer,
and to live faithfully in response to your call.
Through Christ, our Lord. **Amen.**

4 COMPLETE MODEL OUTLINES AND PRAYERS

A basic structure for prayers of the people includes an address to God, praise and thanksgiving for who God is and what God has done, intercessions for local and worldwide concerns, and a concluding doxology.

Prayer Outlines

The following text expands upon the basic structure of intercessory prayer, listing particular areas for intercession. Consider printing this outline for your congregation and filling in particular concerns appropriate to the theme of the worship service and concerns of the moment. Worshipers will be able to sense the scope and flow of the prayer, and they may choose a similar outline for their daily personal and family prayers.

This outline not only encourages spontaneous prayer but also disciplines that spontaneity to maintain a balanced diet of thanksgiving and petition by encouraging prayer leaders to include references to specific events and concerns in the life of the community.

1   (a) Address to God
     (b) Praise and thanksgiving for who God is and what God has done
          (1) in creating the world
          (2) in redeeming the world in Christ
          (3) for specific acts of faithfulness to the present community
          (4) for the sure promise of the coming kingdom
     (c) Intercessions for worldwide and local concerns, including
          (1) the creation and its care, especially ...
          (2) the nations of the world, especially ...
          (3) the nation and those in authority, especially ...
          (4) the community and those who govern, especially ...
          (5) the church universal, its mission, and those who minister,
              especially ...
          (6) the local congregation and its ministry, especially ...
          (7) those with particular needs, especially ...
     (d) Doxology in praise to the triune God,
         in unity with those who praise God in heaven and on earth

The following model prayer is developed in three parts: praise and thanksgiving, petition, and concluding affirmation and doxology. This model supplies helpful phrases for each section of the prayer and allows the leader to improvise within each section.

2   We praise you, God our creator, for your handiwork
     in shaping and sustaining your wondrous creation.
     We especially thank you for
          the miracle of life and the wonder of living ...
          particular blessings coming to us in this day ...
          the resources of the earth ...
          gifts of creative vision and skillful craft ...
          the treasure stored in every human life. . . .

     We pray for others, God our Savior,
     claiming your love in Jesus Christ for the whole world
     and committing ourselves to care for those around us in his name.
     We especially pray for
          those who work for the benefit of others ...
          those who cannot work today ...
          those who teach and those who learn ...
          people who are poor ...
          the church in persecution. . . .

     God our creator,
     yours is the morning, and yours is the evening.
     Let Christ, the sun of righteousness,
     shine forever in our hearts
     and draw us to the light of your radiant glory.
     We ask this for the sake of Jesus Christ, our Redeemer. **Amen.**

Complete Prose Prayers

The following examples provide complete prayers developed in the voice of one person or of the community. They can serve as models to be adapted to a congregation's particular needs.

3   We praise and thank you, O Lord,
    that you have fed us with your Word [*and at your table*].
    Grateful for your gifts and mindful of the communion of your saints,
    we offer to you our prayers for all people.

    God of compassion,
    we remember before you
    the poor and the afflicted,
    the sick and the dying,
    prisoners and all who are lonely,
    the victims of war, injustice, and inhumanity,
    and all others who suffer from whatever their sufferings may be called.
    [*Silence*]

    O Lord of providence
    holding the destiny of the nations in your hand,
    we pray for our country.
    Inspire the hearts and minds of our leaders
    that they, together with all our nation,
    may first seek your kingdom and righteousness
    so that order, liberty, and peace may dwell with your people.
    [*Silence*]

    O God the Creator,
    we pray for all nations and peoples.
    Take away the mistrust and lack of understanding
    that divide your creatures;
    increase in us the recognition that we are all your children.
    [*Silence*]

    O Savior God,
    look upon your church in its struggle upon the earth.
    Have mercy on its weakness,
    bring to an end its unhappy divisions,
    and scatter its fears.
    Look also upon the ministry of your church.
    Increase its courage, strengthen its faith,
    and inspire its witness to all people,
    even to the ends of the earth.
    [*Silence*]

    Author of grace and God of love,
    send your Holy Spirit's blessing to your children here present.
    Keep our hearts and thoughts in Jesus Christ, your Son, our only Savior,
    who has taught us to pray: [*Lord's Prayer*]

4   Sovereign God, King of creation,
     you are the one who has spread out the expanse of the heavens
     and dug the depths of the lakes and seas.
     You are the one who has forested the earth
     and stocked land and sea with swarms of your creatures.
     You called human beings forward to bear your image,
     caring for creation, caring for each other, thriving in the light of your love.
     We confess to you, holy God, that we have often spoiled your gifts,
     abusing creation, ignoring each other, turning our backs on your love.
     Because we did not make ourselves,
     cannot keep ourselves, and could never forgive ourselves,
     we turn to you, our Creator, Savior, and Keeper.
     We bring you thanks for Sabbath rest,
     for a break from work, for this place and these friends,
     for your Word that may be opened and preached into our lives,
     for your name on the lips of people we respect.
     We thank you, O God, that we may wake refreshed from a night's sleep,
     alert to the possibilities of a new day,
     ready for your gifts to find and bless us.
     We bring you thanks, O God,
     for nourishing food and nourishing friends,
     for sunny, unspoiled toddlers and for elderly veterans, rich with wisdom.
     We give you thanks, O God,
     for work to do and energy to do it,
     for fine arts and fine artists
     in all their beauty and skill.
     We give you thanks, O God,
     for sports and games, for patriots and heroes, for wonderful things to read.
     Even on the rainiest Monday morning of our lives
     we have reason to thank you, to bless you, and
     to turn our faces toward the radiance of your love.
     O God, especially for your grace, for your amazing grace—
     so old, so new, always reminding us of our dependence on you,
     always healing with your mercy—
     for your grace we give you thanks, O God.
     Care for our restless world, we pray.
     In your mercy, cool our hotspots,
     restrain the lawless, and stimulate the imagination of peacemakers.
     Defend the weak, heal the sick, and send forth prophets
     who preach good news to the poor.
     We pray, O God, for the church across the world.
     Revive the church, O God, and make us strong
     so that we may serve your purposes,
     add luster to your reputation,
     and bring joy into all the precincts of heaven.
     Take into your care, Lord God, those of us who have been betrayed.
     Blend in us justice and love that stands like flint against unholy deeds
     but also reaches and yearns for unholy persons to become holy.

When we stiffen against your grace, soften us.
When we sag under the weight of our duty, stiffen us.
O God, we did not make ourselves,
cannot keep ourselves,
and could never forgive ourselves.
So we turn to you, our Maker, Provider, and Savior
through Jesus Christ, in whom we pray. **Amen.**

5   O Lord and Father of the household of faith,
we thank you for the gift of faith
worked within us by your Holy Spirit.
We thank you for having called us to yourself,
for consecrating us to your service,
for having set us apart to the sacred ministry of prayer.

O Lord and Father of the household of faith,
we pray for the church
in all her breadth and variety,
gathered out of every nation, family, people, and tongue,
to be a kingdom of priests serving you.
We pray for the church in all the world,
for churches in North America, Europe, and the Middle East,
for churches in Africa, Asia, and Latin America,
for young churches and old churches,
small churches and large churches,
weak churches and strong churches.
Grant to the church true lowliness
and genuine humility where there is pride, unity where there is division.
Grant to her truth where there is error and wisdom where there is folly,
that you might fulfill your purposes for her.

O Lord and Father of the household of faith,
we pray for those stewards to whom you have
entrusted the affairs of your house,
for pastors, elders, deacons, lay leaders, volunteers, and committees.
Give them the spirit of willing service and true humility.
Give them a sense of spiritual devotion.
Give them delight in those whom they serve.
Grant that they may lead your people in the way of Christ,
that thereby we might all enter the land of our heritage.

O Lord and Father of the household of faith,
we pray for all peoples of all nations.
We pray that in every land there might be peace and true justice
(especially in [*country*] and other places of conflict).
Grant that in our own communities
those who are troubled,
those who suffer,
those who are discouraged

might find support in time of need
especially from your church.
Particularly we remember before you
the work done for the troubled, the suffering, and the discouraged
by the deacons in our congregations
and denominational and Christian agencies.

O Lord and Father of the household of faith,
we pray for our nation and
those who lead the nation:
   the president/prime minister and advisors,
   the congress/parliament and the courts,
   the diplomatic corps as they negotiate for peace and justice.
We pray for the leaders of all nations,
that they might know that you have called them
to serve their people in your fear and
for your glory and the good of the peoples.

O Lord and Father of the household of faith,
we pray for those who have special needs.
To all who suffer any sickness or weakness [*especially names(s)*],
   give health and strength.
To all who are disturbed or troubled, give rest and understanding.
To all who are lonely and alienated, give fellowship and love.
To all who grieve and sorrow [*especially name(s)*],
   give comfort and assurance.
To all who are aged and frail, give homes of comfort and safety,
and others to help them, and a willingness to accept help.

All these requests we present to you,
O Father of mercy, in the name of Jesus Christ,
who even now is seated at your right hand to intercede for us
and who will come at the last trumpet to gather us into
his holy city, the Jerusalem that is above,
and toward which we journey even now. **Amen.**

6   Almighty God, gracious Father,
in the presence of your bounty keep us humble,
in the presence of all people's needs make us compassionate and caring.

Give us faith in our praying and love in our serving,
knowing that by your power
all may find a new balance in living and a new victory in adversity.

We pray for all unhappy lives,
those who are bitter and resentful, feeling life has given them a raw deal,
those who are sensitive to criticism and quick to take offense,
those who desire their own way, whatever the inconvenience
   or cost to others.
May your judgment and mercy be for their healing.

We pray for those who are lonely,
who are shy and self-conscious,
who find it hard to make friends;
those who are nervous and timid,
who ever feel themselves strangers in a world they can scarcely understand.
May your presence inspire confidence and ensure companionship.

We pray for those who live with bitter regrets,
for loving relationships brought to ruin,
for opportunities freely given and woefully abused,
for the bitterness of defeat or betrayal at another's hand,
or for failure in personal integrity.
May your grace give new hope to find victory in the very scene of failure.

We pray for all in illness and pain,
weary of the day and fearful of the night.
Grant healing, if it be your will,
and at all times through faith the gift of your indwelling peace.

Bless the company of Christ's folk, the church in every land.
Make her eager in worship,
fearless in proclamation of the gospel, and passionate for caring.

Bless our country. Bless our leaders.
Bless our children and grant us peace within our borders.
Grant us as a nation to be found effective in establishing peace
    throughout the world.

Bless us, each one, in the communion of the saints,
and keep us ever mindful of the great cloud of witnesses that,
following in their steps, as they did in the steps of the Master,
we may with them at the last receive the fulfillment
    promised to your people.
Through Jesus Christ, our Lord. **Amen.**

7   O great God, glorify yourself in all the earth.
Be glorified in creation, be glorified in your church,
be glorified in our worship here this very morning.
Though we are so small and you are so grand,
help us nevertheless to magnify your name.
Help us to make your name and the nature of your grace
larger and easier for people to see.
Help us to live and to worship in such a way
that we become like magnifying glasses
through which our neighbors and coworkers and children and friends
can see you come into focus in ways they may not have seen before.
When people ask for an explanation of the hope we have,
give us the words to answer thoughtfully and well.
When people wonder out loud who Jesus is and why he matters,
help us to reply in words that will echo the sweetness of your gospel.
Help us to magnify your name, O Lord,
so that you may be glorified in all the earth.

Father, ours is a world that could use more glimpses of glory
and fewer glimpses of the hell to which our sin so easily leads.
Ours is a world that needs more of the gentle words of your Son, Jesus,
and fewer angry words shouted by ruthless dictators on platforms
or by husbands who raise both voice and fist against women
        they vowed once to cherish.
We need your glory, Lord God, so that we can aspire to be more like you
and less like the selfish, self-indulgent creatures we have become in our sin.
We need the glory of your grace in a world bent on revenge,
the glory of your truth in a world in love with lies,
the glory of your holiness in a world filled with tawdriness,
the glory of your resurrection life in a world mired in death.
Make us transparent to you so that,
because of your Spirit at work in us,
this world can become a better place,
a more kingdom-like place, a shalom place.

Bless our congregation.
Heal those who are ill;
comfort those who are grieving;
reassure those who feel troubled
and frightened by what the future may hold.
Bless the leadership of our congregation.
Anoint them by your Spirit, and may they really feel that anointing.
As they do sometimes difficult, sometimes joyful, but always holy work,
may they sense your anointing.
Be in the words they speak, the cards they send, the visits they make;
be in the meetings they attend and the committees they work on.
Make each worker in this place a bearer of Pentecost's flame,
warming hearts, providing hope, lending comfort,
and so in all these ways contributing to your glory in this congregation.

Be with all of us as we continue to worship you now
and as we prepare ourselves for the week ahead.
For those of us who need to travel this week—
be it a long trip or many trips across town—grant safety.
For children who climb aboard buses and study at school,
be with them and keep them safe
even as they day by day deepen their awareness
of the world of wonders you have made, Creator God.
For college students writing papers and taking exams,
give them fresh recall of what they have labored so hard to learn.
And for any here today who face an anxious week,
grant extra measures of your Spirit's presence and balm.
For those who worry and who have much to worry about, lend peace.
For those whose worries have led to ulcers, lend healing and calm.
For little children who have been asked to grow up too quickly
because a parent is sick
or because mommy and daddy can't live together any more,

deal gently with these young ones, heavenly Father.
Scoop them up in your divine arms
so that they will know your embrace on those nights
when they find themselves crying into their pillows.

Be also with all the lonely people.
Be with the widow who has been alone for many years
and who we all think has done so well
but who alone knows how much her heart still aches more days than not.
Be with the one who has so long wanted marriage
but who has not found such companionship,
and for whom the years seem to be slipping away.
Be with divorced people who still cannot believe most days
that their fondest dreams for wedded bliss have been shattered
and who now live with both the regret and the loneliness of it all.
Be with those who so wish they could find someone to talk to but cannot,
those who wait for the phone to ring but it stays silent,
those who work so hard on tasks that no one ever mentions or comments on.
Be with those who are hungry for a word of gratitude that never comes,
those who search crowded rooms for a familiar face
but who can never seem to find a friend.
Be with all the lonely people—
be their friend when this world's friends fail,
be their companion when they feel that they walk life's journey alone,
be their word of kindness and hope
when the world seems able only to be gruff and brusque
as it brushes past lives that don't seem to count.

As we continue our worship now, fill us with yourself.
As we sing, lift us ever higher to yourself.
As we give offerings,
be with us as we enter the rhythm of generosity and grace.
As we turn to Word and sacrament, encounter us with your very self.
Be glorified in all we do.
We pray it ever and only in Jesus' precious name. **Amen.**

8   *A prayer during winter*

O God, whom to know is to love,
and whom to love is to find true life,
you have invited us to pray to you,
so this morning we do that
in and through the good and strong name of Christ Jesus, our Lord.
We thank you that we can be here this morning.
We're grateful that you have kept us safe through a week of work,
of travel, of learning, of play.
We thank you that you have protected many of us on snowy and icy roads
even as we remain glad for the blessing of shelter
during winter months and always.
For furnaces that warm us,

for storm windows that provide a buffer between the cold and us,
for sweaters and blankets we can wrap around ourselves,
for coats and mittens to wear when we do go outdoors—
for all these blessings,
and for the money we have to purchase it all in the first place,
we render to you, our Provider God, our thanks and praise.

But we are mindful too of the many people
in this city and elsewhere whose shelters are inadequate,
if they have a roof over their heads at all.
We summon to mind the ill-clad,
those who cannot pay the gas bill,
those whose mittens are threadbare,
and those whose poorly insulated windows whistle when the wind blows.
We cannot be grateful for the ways you provide for most of us, O Lord,
without praying for your providence in the lives of the needy.
In your good name, help your people always
to be reaching out and in so doing
to be the hands and fingers of you, Father God.

This morning we also thank you for this church
and for the many volunteers who every week devote long hours
to lending an ear to the lonely,
to providing a window on your Word to neighborhood children
who need to know that you are love.
When the fruit on this kind of labor seems difficult to see,
may your Spirit distribute bursts of renewed energy and encouragement.
When frustrating and seemingly insoluble problems present themselves,
grant a wisdom and clarity of vision that can help.

We petition for other needs in this place as well, O Lord.
Continue to be with our sick and suffering members
and many others who feel ravaged by the effects of old age.
Sustain family members who grieve silently as they watch helplessly
what appears to be a growing shadow of Alzheimer's disease
    in the mind of a dear person.
Also be especially merciful to our members
who have been living in the presence of that terrible shadow for a long time,
having already bid farewell to one they still love but can no longer reach.

Be too with the many people of this congregation
who suffer in silence as many days as not.
Stand near those who are haunted by bad memories
or who bear the scars of abuse that happened years ago
but still lingers with fresh effects each new morning.
Fortify those who experience panic attacks,
who feel afraid all the time without knowing why.
Lend light to those who pass their days in gloomy clouds of depression.
Signal your love to those who sometimes feel so frustrated at the way
life is turning out that they scarcely know what to do with themselves.

Be with our young children who wither under the taunts of other children,
who poke fun of their weight or their complexion
or their lisp or their off-brand clothing.
Life in this world is not always a picnic, dear God.
Some days are just plain miserable.
The gospel tells us you understand this firsthand through Jesus, our Lord.
Remind us of this compassion and shower us with your love,
especially on days when the love of other people
seems remote or spotty at best.

Yet there are joys too, and we thank you for those gifts.
There are good days too, and we aim our praise for such times
to you first and foremost.
You, O God, have been our help in the past,
and you are our bright hope for years to come.
Your gospel and the holy supper that seals your Word to us
in a new and fresh way is the bright center of our lives.
So bless us in the balance of this service
[and again this evening when we gather for worship once more.]
You have brought us to the blessing of a new morning.
Grant us your presence, and support us all the day long,
until the shadows lengthen and the evening comes,
and the busy world is hushed, and the fever of life is over,
and our work is done.
Then, in your mercy, grant us a safe lodging, and a holy rest,
and peace at the last.
In the Christ, **Amen.**

9   *A prayer during spring*

Lord of creation, in this springtime season
we come to this place this day to praise you.
Your hands, O God, have fashioned whole worlds of wonder.
Today we mark that divine craftsmanship in the budding of the daffodil.
We see colorful crocuses dotting lawns and gardens
and see in this spectacle your very fingerprints.
So often when we touch things,
we leave behind smudgy residues of our sinfulness.
But when you touch the creation, O Father,
you leave behind bright traces of glory.
You dapple the landscape of our lives
with radiant hues of yellow, deep tones of purple,
and flashes of gold as buds push outward on the edge of a branch.

When we open our mouths,
too often we let them gush forth with curses or words said in irritated anger.
When you open your holy mouth, Lord God,
we hear the chorus of the robin's song,
the warble of the goldfinch,
the pure liquid melody of the cardinal.

There is right now so much that is wrong with this world,
so much that causes us anxiety, fear, and deep sadness.
Yet the springtime renewal of life reminds us
that in your hands there is so much that is right.
Help us to see in this spring
not simply a natural cycle that repeats itself each year,
but instead help us to see deeper down
into the dear promise of the gospel itself.
Help us to see in each daffodil
not a fleeting glimpse of beauty that must soon fade away
but an enduring glimpse of the glory you have promised us and all creatures
because of who Jesus Christ is and what he has done.
Help us to find hope in a hopeless age,
peace in a time of war, joy in a world of sorrow,
cause to sing lyrically in a cacophonous era
of shouting, of confusion, and of chaos.

Receive our thanks for all
that is right, good, proper, and radiant with hope.
But hear our petitions for all
that seems wrong, bad, out of joint, and stinking of suffering.
Abide with our sick.
We pray today also that you will comfort our members
whose lives have become what at times seem to be
no more than a series of setbacks and increasing limitations due to old age.
Give stamina to those who have to hear a child say,
"Mom, you can't drive the car anymore," or,
"Dad, we think a move to the nursing section is best for you."
For those who feel their dignity has been stripped,
clothe their spirits with your Spirit,
assuring them that they bear the dignity of being
a child of the great King—a status nothing and no one can remove.
Remind them that nothing can separate them from your love
that is in Christ Jesus, not even old age and the winding down of life.

Be with all in our society who exist
on the dim margins of our collective consciousness.
Provide light for those who so often stumble in the darkness.
Grant healing and proper medical care
for the chronically sick, for the addicted, for the abused.
Help us collectively in church and society
to find food for the hungry, especially for children,
and clothing for the ill-clad.
Give us both the clarity of vision that helps us to see people's needs,
and the wisdom to meet those needs in meaningful and lasting ways.

Bring peace at long last in all places
that for too long have known only war and rumors of war.
Where there is stubborn resolve and tunnel vision

on both sides of this or that divide,
soften hearts and expand vision, O Lord.
Where there is hatred that simmers all the time,
boiling over at times in the form of
a tank smashing the house of the innocent or
a person blowing herself up to kill the innocent,
end this insanity by the sane direction of your Spirit, O God.
Too often we seem to see no way out of various spiraling conflicts.
But we've faced this before, Lord of history.
We prayed for apartheid to end, and it did.
We prayed for the Berlin Wall to fall, and it did.
We prayed for these things,
though we confess we didn't really think we'd live to see the day.
So also we pray for peace
even as we own up to the sneaking suspicion in the back of our minds
that peace seems forever to elude so many parts of this globe.
So surprise us again, Father.
Work through our prayers for a greater justice,
a greater respect for life on all sides,
and a greater peace—all greater than we can even imagine.

Now, O great God, bless us also in the balance of this service,
in our fellowship time and education classes that follow,
in time spent with family this afternoon.
Where we fail to be attentive to the voice of your Spirit,
even as we profess to be focused on you in worship, forgive us.
Still, touch us this day so that we will feel the energy we need
to press on in faithful discipleship in the week ahead.
Lift our sight higher so that we can strive
toward loftier goals in the coming days.
Remind us of your abiding love and grace
so that we can become beacons of love and grace
to coworkers, neighbors, friends, fellow students.
Anoint our eyes to see your image
residing deep within each person we meet.
Anoint our ears to hear the cries
of all who surround us, especially the needy.
Anoint our hands to do gospel work.
Anoint our lips to speak gospel peace
so that in all ways, in all times, in all places, we may glorify you.
In the name of Christ Jesus alone we are so bold to pray this. **Amen.**

Prayers Based on the Lord's Prayer

When the disciples asked Jesus to teach them to pray, he did not lecture about the principles of effective prayer. Instead he gave them a model, drawn largely from prayer themes already familiar to devout Jews of the time. The Lord's Prayer remains the model prayer for all Christians. It teaches us that what we ask of God must be rooted in praise and blessing ("hallowed be your name") and must flow out of the most basic of Christian desires—that God's kingdom come and God's will be done. One way to structure intercessory prayer is to follow the outline of the Lord's Prayer, adding appropriate petitions throughout.

Note that the wording of the Lord's Prayer may vary in the following texts, depending on the wording found in various Bible versions. You may wish to change the wording in some of these prayers to match your version of choice.

10 Our Father in heaven, hallowed be your name. . . .
[*prayers of adoration and thanksgiving*]

Your kingdom come. Your will be done, on earth as it is in heaven. . . .
[*prayers of longing for God's shalom*]

Give us this day our daily bread. . . .
[*prayers for the needs of the community*]

Forgive us our debts, as we also have forgiven our debtors. . . .
[*prayers for interpersonal reconciliation*]

And do not bring us to the time of trial, but rescue us from the evil one. . . .
[*prayers for the world and for personal struggles with temptation and evil*]

For the kingdom and the power and the glory are yours forever. **Amen.**
—based on Matthew 6:13, NRSV

11 *This example includes phrases from the Heidelberg Catechism as extrapolations on each petition of the Lord's Prayer.*

Our Father in heaven,
hallowed be your name.
Help us to really know you,
to bless, worship, and praise you
for all your works
and for all that shines forth from them:
your almighty power, wisdom, kindness,
justice, mercy, and truth.
Help us to direct all our living—
what we think, say, and do—
so that your name will never be blasphemed because of us
but always honored and praised.

Your kingdom come.
Rule us by your Word and Spirit in such a way
that more and more we submit to you.
Keep your church strong, and add to it.
Destroy the devil's work;
destroy every force that revolts against you
and every conspiracy against your Word.
Do this until your kingdom is so complete and perfect
that in it you are all in all.

Your will be done on earth as in heaven.
Help us and all people
to reject our own wills
and to obey your will without any back talk.
Your will alone is good.
Help us one and all to carry out the work we are called to,
as willingly and faithfully as the angels in heaven.

Give us today our daily bread.
Do take care of all our physical needs
so that we come to know
that you are the only source of everything good,
and that neither our work and worry
nor your gifts
can do us any good without your blessing.
And so help us to give up our trust in creatures
and to put trust in you alone.

Forgive us our debts,
as we also have forgiven our debtors.
Because of Christ's blood,
do not hold against us, poor sinners that we are,
any of the sins we do
or the evil that constantly clings to us.
Forgive us, just as we are fully determined,
as evidence of your grace in us,
to forgive our neighbors.

And lead us not into temptation,
but deliver us from the evil one.
By ourselves we are too weak
to hold our own even for a moment.
And our sworn enemies—
the devil, the world, and our own flesh—
never stop attacking us.
And so, Lord,
uphold us and make us strong
with the strength of your Holy Spirit,
so that we may not go down to defeat
in this spiritual struggle,
but may firmly resist our enemies
until we finally win the complete victory.

For yours is the kingdom and the power
and the glory forever.
We have made all these requests of you
because, as our all-powerful King,
you not only want to,
but are able to give us all that is good;
and because your holy name,

and not we ourselves,
should receive all the praise, forever.
It is even more sure that you listen to our prayer,
than that we really desire what we pray for. **Amen.**
  —based on Heidelberg Catechism, Q&A's 119, 122-129

12   *A prayer based on the Lord's Prayer and the Psalms*

Our Father in heaven,
you indeed are our Father, adopting us into an eternal family.
As an earthly father has compassion on his children,
so you show compassion on those who fear you.
You know how we are made, and remember us in our weakness. [Ps. 103]

Hallowed be your name.
You alone are holy, there is none like you;
your glory is above the heavens.
Yet you stoop down to lift up the needy.
We exalt and worship you, for you are holy. [Ps. 113, 99]

Your kingdom come, your will be done, on earth as it is in heaven.
In Christ your kingdom has already come,
even though rulers of this earth
gather together against you,
thinking they can thwart your purposes.
They cannot, for you have installed Christ, your Anointed One,
the everlasting, all powerful King over all creation. [Ps. 2]

Give us this day our daily bread.
All creatures look to you for their food at the proper time;
when you provide, they are satisfied with good things.
When you hide your face, they are terrified.
Lord, help us be good stewards of the gifts of food you have given us
so that all may have their daily bread. [Ps. 104]

Forgive us our sins, as we also forgive those who sin against us.
Blessed are those whose transgressions are forgiven,
whose sin is covered, and who know the joy of forgiveness. [Ps. 32]
As we have been forgiven, help us to become like Christ,
forgiving those who sin against us.

Save us from the time of trial and deliver us from evil.
In mercy, O God, answer the prayers of all who are in deep distress.
Hear their cries especially when they are tormented
by those who deny you and act as if you do not care.
At the same time, save us from sinning in our anger.
Let the light of your face shine upon us, O Lord. [Ps. 4]

**For the kingdom, the power, and glory are yours,
now and forever. Amen.**

Scripture Paraphrase Prayers

The following prayers are based on particular scriptural texts. Some are close paraphrases of actual scriptural prayers, such as psalms. Others are new prayers built on an image or a theme from a biblical text. These are provided as models of an approach that may be used in conjunction with any Scripture text.

13 Lord, our Lord, you are so awesome!
You are beyond what we can imagine possible.
When we take a look at all that you have done and all that you have made,
we wonder why you care for people like us.
You have given us an honorable position on this earth of ours—
to care for the things you have made, to preserve them and maintain them.
You have entrusted living things to us!
Lord, our Lord, the whole earth recognizes how awesome you are!
Amen.
    —based on Psalm 8

14 O Lord, we praise you with all our soul.
We praise you for the abundance of grace and mercy
that we unconsciously receive from you in so many different ways.
You overlook our iniquities.
You bring us back to good health.
You save us from evil and inundate us with your love and compassion.

Lord, you provide nourishment and rejuvenation
to our bodies, minds, and souls.
We also know, Lord, that through you,
there will be justice for the suffering of your people.

Thank you for graciously revealing yourself
to your children so long ago,
that we might have the privilege of knowing your will.

We are only deserving of eternal death as a result of our evil ways.
However, rather than eternally condemning your children in anger,
you bestow your unconditional and boundless love on us.
Through your incomprehensible love for us,
you free us completely from the price of our transgressions.

We cherish your compassion
just as a child cherishes the compassion of loving parents.
We know that, without your compassion,
we would be reduced to nothing but dust on this material planet,
alive and growing one day,
then dead and blown away with the wind the next,
fading away even from human memories forever.
Because of your compassion, Lord, we are allowed a life of eternity;
a gift that you have promised even to future God-fearing generations.
Help us and all future generations to hold tightly
to your precious covenant through obedience to your will.

Lord, from your mighty throne you rule over us all.
We call the cherubim that surround you, the seraphim that serve you,
and every believer in your domain to join our souls
in praising your holy name! **Amen.**
    —based on Psalm 103

15 No matter where we are, where we are going, or what we are doing,
we know that we find our help in you, our Lord.
You are the creator and sustainer of all
that has been made and will be made.
And yet, the immensity of creation does not distract you
from caring personally for every person in it.

We know that is true of your care for us too!
You do not daydream or become weary in that care.
We thank you that you not only watch over us with diligence
but that you will guide us so that we will not fall—
so that we won't even stumble.

Whether we are awake or asleep, you are there,
sheltering and protecting us from all that would hurt us.
We know that you watch over all our living—
you have in the past, and we know you are now.
Your promise holds for the future and for eternity,
and we praise and thank you for that. **Amen.**
    —based on Psalm 121

16 Praise the Lord!
Our soul praises you, O Lord.
We will sing praises to you as long as we live.
We will not put our trust in our government or in influential people,
for when they die, their influence and power are gone.

We are blessed because we hope and trust in you,
O God who created the world and everything in it.
You were a faithful God to our spiritual fathers, Abraham, Isaac, and Jacob,
and you remain unchanging and faithful to us in this century
and on to the end of time.

You uphold those of us
who are weighed down with the cares of this world,
and you feed those who are hungry with the bread of life.
You set prisoners free with the assurance that their sins are forgiven
and that you are in control of the events of their lives.
You give sight of understanding to those who are blind in their sin.
You lift up those who are bowed down,
and you love those who are righteous.

You watch over us aliens in a sinful world,
and you are a father to the orphaned and a comforter to the widowed.
You do not allow the plans of the wicked

to flourish or to come to completion.
You will reign forever and for all generations.
Praise the Lord! **Amen.**
—based on Psalm 146

17   Lord Jesus, you are our living head.
Teach us to be your body here on earth—
your hands, your feet, your eyes, and your compassionate heart.
Lord, send the impulses of your love into the sinews of this church.
May your will and thoughts direct us.
Let your hands, through our hands, supply food for our neighbors' hunger.
Let them hear your voice as we visit and talk with them.
Let children come to us and sit in our laps, as they sat in yours.
Without you as our head, Lord, we are lifeless.
We wait for your power, your Word, your instruction.
Fill us with your life and love, Jesus. **Amen.**
—based on 1 Corinthians 12:12-31

Prayers in Litany Form

A litany is a prayer led by one person with responses by the congregation. The responses may be extended prose, but they are usually a repeated refrain, such as "Lord, hear our prayer" or "Lord, have mercy upon us." The responses may also be sung. The congregation's response should be clearly introduced by the leader or indicated in a printed order of worship.

18   Gracious God,
we pray for the faithful all over the world,
that all who love you may be united in your service.
We pray for the church . . .
Lord, in your mercy,
hear our prayer.

We pray for the peoples and leaders of the nations,
that they may be reconciled one to another
in pursuit of your justice and peace.
We pray for the world . . .
Lord, in your mercy,
hear our prayer.

We pray for all who suffer from prejudice, greed, or violence,
that the heart of humanity may warm with your tenderness.
We pray especially for all prisoners of politics or religion
and for all refugees.
We pray for all who are oppressed . . .
Lord, in your mercy,
hear our prayer.

We pray for all in need
because of famine, flood, or earthquake,
that they may know the hope of your faithfulness
through the help of others.
We pray especially for the people of . . .
Lord, in your mercy,
hear our prayer.

We pray for the land, the sea, the sky—
for your whole creation, which longs for its redemption.
We pray that we may live with respect for your creation
and use your gifts with reverence.
We pray for the creation . . .
Lord, in your mercy,
hear our prayer.

We pray for all who suffer the pain of sickness,
loneliness, fear, or loss,
that those whose names are in our hearts,
in the hearts of others,
or known to you alone,
may receive strength and courage.
We pray for those in need . . .
Lord, in your mercy,
hear our prayer.

God of compassion,
into your hands we commend all for whom we pray,
trusting in your mercy now and forever. **Amen.**

19 Let us bring the needs of the church,
the world, and all in need, to God's loving care.
Please respond to the words, "Lord, in your mercy,"
by saying "hear our prayer."

God of heaven and earth,
through Jesus Christ you promise to hear us
when we pray to you in his name.
Confident in your love and mercy
we offer our prayer.
Lord, in your mercy,
hear our prayer.

Empower the church throughout the world in its life and witness.
Break down the barriers that divide
so that, united in your truth and love,
the church may confess your name,
share one baptism,
sit together at one table,
and serve you in one common ministry.
Lord, in your mercy,
hear our prayer.

Guide the rulers of the nations.
Move them to set aside their fear, greed, and vain ambition
and to bow to your sovereign rule.
Inspire them to strive for peace and justice,
that all your children may dwell secure,
free of war and injustice.
Lord, in your mercy,
hear our prayer.

Hear the cries of the world's hungry and suffering.
Give us, who consume most of the earth's resources,
the will to reorder our lives,
that all may have their rightful share of food,
medical care, and shelter,
and so have the necessities of a life of dignity.
Lord, in your mercy,
hear our prayer.

Restore among us a love of the earth you created for our home.
Help us put an end to ravishing its land, air, and waters,
and give us respect for all your creatures,
that, living in harmony with everything you have made,
your whole creation may resound in an anthem of praise
to your glorious name.
Lord, in your mercy,
hear our prayer.

Renew our nation in the ways of justice and peace.
Guide those who make and administer our laws
to build a society based on trust and respect.
Erase prejudices that oppress;
free us from crime and violence;
guard our youth from the perils of drugs and materialism.
Give all citizens a new vision of a life of harmony.
Lord, in your mercy,
hear our prayer.

Strengthen this congregation in its work and worship.
Fill our hearts with your self-giving love,
that our voices may speak your praise
and our lives may conform to the image of your Son.
Nourish us with your Word and sacraments,
that we may faithfully minister in your name
and witness to your love and grace for all the world.
Lord, in your mercy,
hear our prayer.

Look with compassion on all who suffer.
Support with your love
those with incurable and stigmatized diseases,
those unjustly imprisoned,

those denied dignity,
those who live without hope,
those who are homeless or abandoned.
As you have moved toward us in love,
so lead us to be present with them in their suffering
in the name of Jesus Christ.
Lord, in your mercy,
hear our prayer.

Sustain those among us who need your healing touch.
Make the sick whole [*especially name(s)*].
Give hope to the dying [*especially name(s)*].
Comfort those who mourn [*especially name(s)*].
Uphold all who suffer in body or mind,
not only those we know and love
but also those known only to you,
that they may know the peace and joy of your supporting care.
Lord, in your mercy,
hear our prayer.

O God,
in your loving purpose
answer our prayers and fulfill our hopes.
In all things for which we pray,
give us the will to seek to bring them about,
for the sake of Jesus Christ. **Amen.**

20 *The following traditional prayer, based on Eastern Orthodox tradition, is often attributed to St. John Chrysostom.*

In peace, let us pray to the Lord.
Lord, hear our prayer.

For the peace from above,
for the loving-kindness of God,
and for our salvation,
let us pray to the Lord.
Lord, hear our prayer.

For the peace of the world,
for the unity of the church of God,
and for the well-being of all peoples,
let us pray to the Lord.
Lord, hear our prayer.

For this gathering of the faithful,
and for all who offer here
their worship and praise,
let us pray to the Lord.
Lord, hear our prayer.

For all the baptized,
for all who serve in the church,
[*for (names)*],
let us pray to the Lord.
Lord, hear our prayer.

For our elected officials,
for the leaders of the nations,
and for all in authority,
let us pray to the Lord.
Lord, hear our prayer.

For this city [*town, village, etc.*],
for every city and community,
and for those who live in them,
let us pray to the Lord.
Lord, hear our prayer.

For seasonable weather,
and for abundant harvests for all to share,
let us pray to the Lord.
Lord, hear our prayer.

For the good earth that God has given us,
and for the wisdom and will to conserve it,
let us pray to the Lord.
Lord, hear our prayer.

For those who travel by land, water, or air
[*or through outer space*],
let us pray to the Lord.
Lord, hear our prayer.

For those who are aged and infirm,
for those who are widowed and orphaned,
and for those who are sick and suffering,
let us pray to the Lord.
Lord, hear our prayer.

For those who are poor and oppressed,
for those who are unemployed and destitute,
for those who are imprisoned and captive,
and for all who remember and care for them,
let us pray to the Lord.
Lord, hear our prayer.

For deliverance in times of affliction,
strife, and need,
let us pray to the Lord.
Lord, hear our prayer.

Almighty God,
you have given us grace at this time with one accord
to make our common supplication to you,
and you have promised through your well-beloved Son
that when two or three are gathered together in his name
you will be in the midst of them.
Fulfill now, O Lord, our desires and petitions
as may be best for us,
granting us in this world knowledge of your truth,
and in the age to come life everlasting. Amen.

21   Lord God,
because Jesus has taught us to trust you in all things,
we hold to his Word and share his plea:
Your kingdom come, your will be done.

Where nations budget for war,
while Christ says, "Put up your sword":
Your kingdom come, your will be done.

Where countries waste food and covet fashion,
while Christ says, "I was hungry . . . I was thirsty . . .":
Your kingdom come, your will be done.

Where powerful governments
claim their policies are heaven blessed,
while Scripture states that God helps the powerless:
Your kingdom come, your will be done.

Where Christians seek the kingdom
in the shape of their own church,
as if Christ had come to build
and not to break barriers:
Your kingdom come, your will be done.

Where women who speak up for their dignity
are treated with scorn or contempt:
Your kingdom come, your will be done.

Where men try hard to be tough,
because they are afraid to be tender:
Your kingdom come, your will be done.

Where we, obsessed with being adults,
forget to become like children:
Your kingdom come, your will be done.

Where our prayers falter,
our faith weakens,
our light grows dim:
Your kingdom come, your will be done.

Where Jesus Christ calls us:
Your kingdom come, your will be done.

Lord God,
you have declared that your kingdom is among us.
Open our ears to hear it,
our hands to serve it,
our hearts to hold it.
This we pray in Jesus' name. **Amen.**

22   Let us pray for the church and for the world.

Grant, Almighty God, that all who confess your name
may be united in your truth, live together in your love, and reveal your glory in the
world.
[*Silence*]
Lord, in your mercy,
hear our prayer.

Guide the people of this land, and of all the nations,
in the ways of justice and peace,
that we may honor one another and serve the common good.
[*Silence*]
Lord, in your mercy,
hear our prayer.

Give us all a reverence for the earth as your own creation,
that we may use its resources rightly in the service of others
and to your honor and glory.
[*Silence*]
Lord, in your mercy,
hear our prayer.

Bless all whose lives are closely linked with ours,
and grant that we may serve Christ in them
and love one another as he loves us.
[*Silence*]
Lord, in your mercy,
hear our prayer.

Comfort and heal all who suffer in body, mind, or spirit.
Give them courage and hope in their troubles,
and bring them the joy of your salvation.
[*Silence*]
Lord, in your mercy,
hear our prayer.

Almighty and eternal God, ruler of all things in heaven and earth,
mercifully accept the prayers of your people
and strengthen us to do your will
through Jesus Christ, our Lord. **Amen.**

Bidding Prayers

One type of litany or responsive prayer has traditionally been known as "bidding prayer." In this form of prayer the leader invites, or "bids," worshipers to pray for a particular subject; the worshipers respond with either silent or extemporaneously spoken prayers; then the leader concludes with a brief summary prayer. This pattern may be repeated as many times as appropriate for several topics or subjects of prayer.

23 Bound together in Christ in the communion of the Holy Spirit,
let us pray with one heart and mind to our God, saying:
God of all mercies,
hear our prayer. [*or* **Triune God, hear us.**]

That the love that passes ceaselessly
between the Father and the Son in the fellowship of the Holy Spirit
may renew and deepen the life of each Christian
and draw us all gathered here into your unending life, we pray:
God of all mercies,
hear our prayer. [*or* **Triune God, hear us.**]

For the leaders of the church [*especially (names)*]
and for the leaders of nations [*especially name(s)*],
that they may discern ways to overcome divisions and mistrust
and may reflect your unity in every aspect of common life, we pray:
God of all mercies,
hear our prayer. [*or* **Triune God, hear us.**]

For our families, our households, and our communities,
that they may be places of communion and mutual support,
which build us up and strengthen us in grace and truth, we pray:
God of all mercies,
hear our prayer. [*or* **Triune God, hear us.**]

Thankful for our world that you made through Christ
and renewed in the power of the resurrection,
that we may be wise and careful stewards of creation, we pray:
God of all mercies,
hear our prayer. [*or* **Triune God, hear us.**]

In the power of the Spirit,
who joins our prayers to Christ's enduring intercession,
we pray for the sick, the suffering,
and all who stand in need [*especially (names)*].
For healing for all the world we pray:
God of all mercies,
hear our prayer. [*or* **Triune God, hear us.**]

[*Here other intercessions may be offered.*]

Gracious God, whom Jesus called Abba, Father,
accept our prayers this day.

By the inner workings of your Spirit, deepen our communion with you,
the source and goal of our life,
and make us more and more signs of your enduring love.
This we pray through Christ, who lives and works
with you and the Holy Spirit, one God, now and forever. **Amen.**

24 *The following prayer may be offered in whole or in part.*

Almighty God,
in Jesus Christ you taught us to pray
and to offer our petitions to you in his name.
Guide us by your Holy Spirit,
that our prayers for others may serve your will
and show your steadfast love,
through the same Jesus Christ, our Lord. **Amen.**

Let us pray for the world.

[*Individual prayers may be offered extemporaneously or in silence.*]

God our creator,
you made all things in your wisdom,
and in your love you save us.
We pray for the whole creation.
Overthrow evil powers, right what is wrong,
feed and satisfy those who thirst for justice,
so that all your children may freely enjoy the earth you have made
and joyfully sing your praises,
through Jesus Christ, our Lord. **Amen.**

Let us pray for the church.

[*Individual prayers may be offered extemporaneously or in silence.*]

Gracious God,
you have called us to be the church of Jesus Christ.
Keep us one in faith and service,
breaking bread together
and proclaiming the good news to the world,
that all may believe you are love,
turn to your ways,
and live in the light of your truth,
through Jesus Christ, our Lord. **Amen.**

Let us pray for peace.

[*Individual prayers may be offered extemporaneously or in silence.*]

Eternal God,
you sent us a Savior, Christ Jesus,
to break down the walls of hostility that divide us.
Send peace on earth,
and put down greed, pride, and anger,
which turn nation against nation and race against race.

Speed the day when wars will end
and the whole world will accept your rule,
through Jesus Christ, our Lord. **Amen.**

Let us pray for our enemies.

[*Individual prayers may be offered extemporaneously or in silence.*]

O God,
whom we cannot love unless we love our neighbors,
remove hate and prejudice from us and from all people,
so that your children may be reconciled
with those we fear, resent, or threaten,
and may live together in your peace,
through Jesus Christ, our Lord. **Amen.**

Let us pray for those who govern us.

[*Individual prayers may be offered extemporaneously or in silence.*]

Mighty God,
sovereign over the nations,
direct those who make, administer, and judge our laws—
the president/prime minister
and others in authority among us [*especially (names)*]—
that, guided by your wisdom,
they may lead us in the way of righteousness,
through Jesus Christ, our Lord. **Amen.**

Let us pray for world leaders.

[*Individual prayers may be offered extemporaneously or in silence.*]

Eternal Ruler, hope of all the earth,
give vision to those who serve the United Nations
and to those who govern all countries,
that, with goodwill and justice,
they may take down barriers
and draw together one new world in peace,
through Jesus Christ, our Lord. **Amen.**

Let us pray for the sick.

[*Individual prayers may be offered extemporaneously or in silence.*]

Merciful God,
you bear the pain of the world.
Look with compassion on those who are sick [*especially (names)*];
cheer them by your Word
and bring healing as a sign of your grace,
through Jesus Christ, our Lord. **Amen.**

Let us pray for those who sorrow.

[*Individual prayers may be offered extemporaneously or in silence.*]

God of comfort,
stand with those who sorrow [*especially (names)*],
that they may be sure that neither death nor life,
nor things present nor things to come,
shall separate them from your love,
through Jesus Christ, our Lord. **Amen.**

Let us pray for friends and families.

[*Individual prayers may be offered extemporaneously or in silence.*]

God of compassion,
bless us and those we love,
our friends and families,
that, drawing close to you,
we may be drawn closer to each other,
through Jesus Christ, our Lord. **Amen.**

[*Other petitions may be added in the same manner.*]

God of all generations,
we praise you for all your servants
who, having been faithful to you on earth,
now live with you in heaven.
Keep us in fellowship with them,
until we meet with all your children
in the joy of your eternal kingdom,
through Jesus Christ, our Lord. **Amen.**

Mighty God,
whose Word we trust,
whose Spirit enables us to pray,
accept our requests
and further those that will bring about your purpose for the earth,
through Jesus Christ, who rules over all things. **Amen.**

25 *After each section of the following prayer, anyone may offer a person's name or a short prayer
for someone to whom the situation applies. Each section may be followed by a spoken or sung
response like the following:*

Lord, draw near,
Lord, draw near,
draw near and stay.

or

Lord, in your mercy,
hear our prayer.

Let us pray for those who need to be
remembered tonight.

Those who have made the news headlines today
because of what they have done or said . . .
[*Response*]

Those who have been brought to our attention
through a meeting or conversation . . .
[*Response*]

Those who are in hospital, in care,
or in a place that is strange to them;
those in whose family, marriage,
or close relationship
there is stress or a break-up . . .
[*Response*]

Those who are waiting for a birth, or a death,
or news that will affect their lives . . .
[*Response*]

Those whose pain or potential
we should not forget to share with God tonight . . .
[*Response*]

Lord, we believe that you hear our prayer
and will be faithful to your promise to answer us.

When our eyes open again,
may they do so not to end our devotions,
but to expect the kingdom,
for Jesus' sake. **Amen.**

26 *At the end of each section of this prayer, worshipers may say aloud the first names of people
they wish to pray for.*

Eternal God,
whom our words may cradle but never contain,
we thank you for all the sound and silence
and color and symbol
that, through the centuries, have helped
the worship of your church
to be relevant and real.
Here we pause to remember those
who helped us to come to faith,
by singing us songs or telling us stories,
by inviting us in when we felt distant,
by praying for us without being asked.
We name them now.
[*Names mentioned aloud, followed by the response:*]
Jesus, Son of God among us,
hear our prayer.

We remember the preachers, the readers,
the musicians, the leaders,
whose sensitivity and skill
have helped us to grow in faith
and to enjoy worshiping you.

We name them now.
[*Names* . . .]
Jesus, Son of God among us,
hear our prayer.

We remember those
who encourage people to praise you
outside the sanctuary:
those who teach young children,
those who lead youth groups,
those who take prayers in hospitals,
    in schools,
    in prisons.
We name them now.
[*Names* . . .]
Jesus, Son of God among us,
hear our prayer.

We remember people who cannot pray
and who struggle to believe,
or who fear changes in the church
more than in any other area of their lives.
We name them now,
praying that they might be encouraged,
and that love might dispel fear.
[*Names* . . .]
Jesus, Son of God among us,
hear our prayer.

And let us pray for the renewal of the church,
beginning with ourselves.
Reshape us, good Lord,
until in generosity,
in faith,
and in expectation
that the best is yet to come,
we are truly Christlike.
Make us passionate followers of Jesus
rather than passive supporters.

Make our churches
communities of radical discipline
and signposts to heaven;
then, in us, through us,
and—if need be—despite us,
let your kingdom come. Amen.

27 In the brief times following each topic of petition,
you are invited to name out loud
or pray in silence for all who have such needs. Let us pray:

for those who are ill, who face surgeries, and those recovering . . .
for those who suffer mental and emotional distress . . .
for those who struggle with addictions . . .
for those who provide health care . . .

for those who are lonely, orphans, and displaced . . .
for those who are poor, hungry, and homeless . . .
for those who are rich and powerful . . .
for those who are imprisoned and those who are persecuted . . .
for those who are unemployed and those who are exploited . . .
for those who provide social services and counsel . . .

for those who live in families or as singles . . .
for those who expect a child or yearn for a child . . .
for those who provide childcare and education . . .
for those who labor in business and government . . .
for those who serve in our armed forces . . .
for those who work in the sciences, arts, and media . . .
for those who are leaders in Christian churches throughout the world . . .
for those who make peace in the world and those who are our enemies . . .

As we offer these petitions,
let us remember before God and each other
how each of us has responsibilities to act upon the prayers we raise.
May our God hear our prayers
and gift us with his Spirit to enable us to be faithful followers of Christ. **Amen.**

Prayers Especially for Children

28 *A prayer especially appropriate for children*

Loving God:
We love the beautiful world you have made: the sun and clouds, the seas and
mountains, plants and animals [include specific items that children suggest].
We thank you for the Bible: for stories of Abraham and Sarah, Moses and Miriam,
and especially those about Jesus [include specific items that children suggest].
We pray today for all whom we love: our parents, teachers, pastors, and friends
[include specific people that children suggest].
We pray especially for all who need your help in a special way: [include specific
items that children suggest].
We pray today for people we do not know: people who live far away, people who
cannot leave the hospital or nursing home [include specific items that children
suggest].
Help us to grow in your love today, as we pray and worship, as we learn from your
Word, as we share your love with others [include specific items that children
suggest].
We pray in Jesus' name. **Amen.**

29 *This prayer is designed to reflect the experience of children and is based on the teaching model above.*

Lord God, thank you for making us part of your family
and for giving us our own families.
Help us to love each other as you love us.
Keep us safe and healthy, and help us to enjoy being with each other.

Thank you for giving us all kinds of people to teach us—
our parents and grandparents,
babysitters and friends,
Sunday school leaders and school teachers,
ministers and many more.
Make them excited about what they teach
and make us all excited about learning more about you.

Lord, we can't even think of all the people who help us each day.
Lead our president/prime minister and government leaders
to make good decisions.
Please keep our firefighters, police officers, and all other people
who work to keep our city safe.
Thank you for these and other strong people who take care of us.

We also pray for people who need help—
for everyone who is sick or scared.
We know you heal better than any doctor on earth.
Give your strength to everyone who is suffering.

We also ask you to bless each of us.
You are the great shepherd who loves us.
Help us to know you will always give us everything we need,
and help us to be happy with what we have.
Continue to watch over us, and teach us to live for you all of the time.
In Jesus' name we pray. **Amen.**

30. Loving God,
thank you for everything,
especially the world you have made for us,
the family and friends you give us,
and the love you show us.
Please help sick people feel better,
sad people feel happier,
and angry people feel friendlier.
Help us to grow bigger, stronger,
and more like you every day.
For Jesus' sake, **Amen.**

5 Prayers on Pastorally Challenging Topics

The following specific topics or themes for prayer serve as a sampling of many topics that are especially difficult or neglected.

Prayers for Justice and Peace

1   Lover of all humankind,
    you call us to be caring and hospitable
    toward strangers in our midst.
    When brothers and sisters from other countries
    flee the difficulties of their land,
    help us to welcome and to walk gently with them.
    When students and visitors from far away
    choose our land as their destination,
    help us to respond in kindness to their interests and needs.
    [*We pray especially for (names/group/committee) as it extends care and goodwill
    to (individual/group) at this time.*]
    May we care for all our neighbors as for ourselves,
    that we may know the blessing of giving. **Amen.**

2   Creator God, convenience and greed have outweighed concern for your world.
    Help your beautiful creation not only to survive but thrive.
    We need you, Lord; listen to our call for help.
    Bread of Life, our world is full of people starving for food or attention.
    Satisfy their needs with your abundance.
    We need you, Lord; listen to our call for help.
    Great Physician, at times insurance or finances
    prohibit the treatment or prevention of disease.
    Free the sick from pain, from unanswered questions, and from nights of worry.
    We need you, Lord; listen to our call for help.
    Peacemaker, our world is torn by political and economic turmoil.
    May we, and your whole world, rest in your everlasting embrace.
    We need you, Lord; listen to our call for help.
    Help of the helpless, the rich and powerful can't always hear the cries of the weak.
    Enable us—whether rich or poor, powerful or powerless—
    to bring comfort and relief to those in need.
    We need you, Lord; listen to our call for help.
    O God, you are forgiving and good, full of love for all who call to you.
    You are our God. You alone can renew our world. Amen.

3   How crooked is our world, O God, and how heavy with sadness:
         the hungry cry out for food; the imprisoned long for freedom;
         the blind want to see; the troubled in heart need relief;
         the alien, the orphaned, and the widow are desperate for help;
         those who stand for what is right want to know their cause is not in vain.
     Show yourself to be God:
         Frustrate the ways of the wicked.
         Sustain the righteous
         and help those who are in need.
     In the name of Jesus Christ and the power of the Holy Spirit. **Amen.**
              —based on Psalm 146

4   As we listen to the world's concerns,
     hear the cry of the oppressed,
     and learn of new discoveries,
     give us knowledge,
     teach us to respond with maturity,
     and give us courage to act with integrity.

     As citizens, we acknowledge the Spirit's work in human government
     for the welfare of the people,
     for justice among the poor,
     for mercy toward the prisoner,
     against inhuman oppression of humanity.
     Help us to obey you above all rulers;
     fill us with the patience of Christ
     as we wait upon the Spirit.
     We pray for the fruit of the Spirit of Christ
     who works for peace on earth,
     commands us to love our enemies,
     and calls for patience among the nations.
     We give thanks for your work among governments,
     seeking to resolve disputes by means other than war,
     placing human kindness above national pride,
     replacing the curse of war with international self-control.

     We hear the Spirit's call to love one another,
     opposing discrimination of race or sex,
     inviting us to accept one another,
     and to share at every level
     in work and play, in church and state,
     in marriage and family, and so to fulfill the love of Christ.
     Enable us to accept that call and be agents of renewal in our work
     through our Lord Jesus Christ. **Amen.**
              —based on *Our Song of Hope*, st. 9-12

5   Father,
    we give our thanks for the men and women
    who go on doing their duty
    in the face of loneliness,
    monotony, misunderstanding, danger.
    We pray for those who serve us in this city at hazard to their lives:
    police and firefighters and all others whose work demands constant risk.
    We pray for soldiers and sailors who at any moment
    are either bored or scared
    but who stay at their post and do what they must.
    Father, bless their courage with the peace that they, and we, are praying for.
    Forgive us, Father, if we ever take for granted what others are doing
    so that we can live in peace and safety.
    Make us the kind of people who appreciate these blessings.
    We expect others to show courage in the line of duty.
    If, once in a while, we must stand up
    and show a little courage of our own,
    help us to set an example by being the kind of people
    Christ has called us to be. **Amen.**

6   Almighty God,
    you have given us this good land as our heritage.
    Help us always to remember your generosity
    and constantly do your will.
    Bless our land with honest industry, sound learning,
    and an honorable way of life.
    Save us from violence, discord, and confusion,
    from pride and arrogance, and from every evil way.
    Defend our liberties and give those whom we have entrusted
    with the authority of government the spirit of wisdom,
    that there might be justice and peace in our land.
    When times are prosperous, let our hearts be thankful;
    in troubled times, do not let our trust in you fail.
    We ask all this through Jesus Christ, our Lord. **Amen.**

7   We pray to you, O Lord, our God and Father,
    because we are encouraged by Jesus Christ,
    your Son and our brother, to do so.
    You have said through the mouth of the prophet:
    "Seek the good of the city and pray for it to the Lord";
    we therefore pray to you today
    for our cities and villages and for the whole land,
    for justice and righteousness, for peace and good order everywhere.
    Have mercy, Lord, we pray.
    We pray for those who govern.
    Teach them that you are the ruler of all
    and that they are only your instruments.

Grant them wisdom for their difficult decisions,
a sharp eye for what is essential,
and courage to obey your commandment.
Have mercy, Lord, we pray.
We pray for all who, by your ordaining,
are responsible for justice and peace.
We pray for all who continue to seek salvation in violence.
Show terrorists that no blessing rests in violence.
Take the young among them especially into your care
and bring order into their confused thoughts.
Bring murder and kidnapping to an end.
Have mercy, Lord, we pray.
We pray for all who are no longer able to sleep in peace
because they fear for their own life
and for the lives of those near and dear to them;
we pray for all who no longer have hope in your kingdom
and for all who are tormented by anxiety or despair.
Grant that they may be blessed
with faithful friends and counselors alongside them
to comfort them with your strengthening gospel and sacrament.
Have mercy, Lord, we pray.
Lord, you have the whole wide world in your hands.
You are able to turn human hearts as seems best to you;
grant your grace therefore to the bonds of peace and love,
and in all lands join together whatever has been torn asunder. **Amen.**

8 From many places, O Lord, we gather today,
brought together in this house of worship.
We come from different backgrounds
and even different countries.
Some of us are new to the faith,
while some of us have been on this journey for a long time.
Yet together we praise you for this place of sanctuary
and for a time to praise your holy name.

Still, our hearts are heavy this day, Lord.
Our world groans with the weight of sin;
we cannot comprehend the evils we see around us;
and we cry with those who today mourn the dead.
May we make a difference in the midst of this sorrow;
may your people around the world rise up against evil;
may we be brought to our knees as we call upon your name;
may your kingdom come quickly, Lord. **Amen.**

Prayers for Healing

9   Let us pray, responding to the phrase,
"Jesus Christ, lover of all,"
with the words, "bring healing, bring peace."

Christ our Lord,
long ago in Galilee,
many who were sick and suffering
needed friends to bring them to your side.
Confident of your goodness,
we now bring to you
those who need your healing touch.
We name before you
those who are ill in body,
whose illness is long, or painful,
or difficult to cure,
those who suffer restless days and sleepless nights.
[*Names of specific individuals may be said aloud.*]
Jesus Christ, lover of all,
bring healing, bring peace.

We name before you
those who are troubled in mind,
distressed by the past,
or dreading the future,
those who are trapped
and cast down by fear.
[*Names of specific individuals may be said aloud.*]
Jesus Christ, lover of all,
bring healing, bring peace.

We name before you
those for whom light has been turned to darkness
by the death of a loved one,
the breaking of a friendship,
or the fading of hope.
[*Names of specific individuals may be said aloud.*]
Jesus Christ, lover of all,
bring healing, bring peace.

In silence we name before you
those whose names we may not say aloud.
[*Silence*]
Jesus Christ, lover of all,
bring healing, bring peace.

We ask your guidance
for those who are engaged in medical research,
that they may persevere with vision and energy;
and for those who administer

agencies of health and welfare,
that they may have wisdom and compassion.
Jesus Christ, lover of all,
bring healing, bring peace. Amen.

10   Most merciful God, you hold each of us dear to your heart.
Hold [*name(s)*] in your loving arms
and tenderly draw them into your love,
together with all who are living with AIDS and HIV infection.
[*Other diseases or suffering of mind, body, or spirit may also be mentioned.*]
Assure them that they are not alone,
and give them the courage and faith for all that is to come.
Strengthen those who care for them and treat them,
and guide those who do research.
Forgive those who have judged harshly,
and enlighten those who live in prejudice and fear.
Nourish those who have lost sight of you,
and heal the spirits of those who are broken.
We pray this in the name of Jesus, who suffered and died,
and then rose from the dead to lead us into new life,
now and forever. **Amen.**

11   Lord Jesus Christ,
we come to you sharing the suffering that you endured.
Grant us patience during this time,
that as we and [*name*]
live with pain, disappointment, and frustration,
we may realize that suffering is a part of life,
a part of life that you know intimately.
Touch [*name*] in his/her time of trial,
hold him/her tenderly in your loving arms,
and let him/her know you care.
Renew us in our spirits,
even when our bodies are not being renewed,
that we might be ever prepared to dwell in your eternal home,
through our faith in you, Lord Jesus,
who died and are alive for evermore. **Amen.**

12   Eternal God, you knew us before we were born
and will continue to know us after we have died.
Touch [*name*] with your grace and presence.
As you give your abiding care,
assure him/her of our love and presence.
Assure him/her that our communion together remains secure,
and that your love for him/her is unfailing.
In Christ, who came to us, we pray. **Amen.**

13 O Christ, our Lord,
in times past many servants of yours
brought their friends and loved ones to your side,
that they might be blessed and healed.
So today we bring to your attention
those who need your loving touch.
Please look on our faith, small as it is, and send your peace.
O Lord, bring your healing and your peace!

We lift up before you
those who suffer from severe physical pain
and those for whom the days are long and the nights seem longer.
O Lord, bring your healing and your peace!

For others, Lord, the pain is not of their body,
but of their mind and emotions.
Some are haunted by past failures;
some feel the searing pain of rejection;
some are shackled with fear and depression;
still others are lonely and alone.
O Lord, bring your healing and your peace!

We also lift before you
those who are crippled in soul and spirit,
who feel that you have abandoned them
or that they are unloved by you.
O Lord, bring your healing and your peace!

We also pray for those who tend the sick,
comfort the dying, care for the poor, and befriend the oppressed.
May their hearts be strong and filled with love and compassion.
When they are weary, infuse the strength of your Spirit.
O Lord, bring your healing and your peace!

This we ask in the name of Jesus Christ,
who came to suffer among us
and to care for those who suffer. **Amen.**

14 Almighty and everlasting God,
who can banish all affliction both of soul and of body,
show forth your power upon those in need,
that by your mercy they may be restored to serve you afresh
in holiness of living, through Jesus Christ, our Lord. **Amen.**

15 God the Father,
your will for all people is health and salvation;
we praise and thank you, O Lord.

God the Son,
you came that we might have life and have it abundantly;
we praise and thank you, O Lord.

God the Holy Spirit,
you make our bodies the temple of your presence;
we praise and thank you, O Lord.

Holy Trinity, one God,
in you we live and move and have our being;
we praise and thank you, O Lord.

Lord, grant your healing grace
to all who are sick, injured, or disabled,
that they may be made whole;
hear us, O Lord of life.

Grant to all who seek your guidance,
and to all who are lonely, anxious, or despondent,
a knowledge of your will and an awareness of your presence;
hear us, O Lord of life.

Mend broken relationships,
and restore those in emotional distress
to soundness of mind and serenity of spirit;
hear us, O Lord of life.

Bless physicians, nurses, and all others who minister to the suffering,
granting them wisdom and skill, sympathy and patience;
hear us, O Lord of life.

Grant to the dying peace and a holy death,
and uphold by the grace and consolation
of your Holy Spirit those who are bereaved;
hear us, O Lord of life.

Restore to wholeness whatever is broken by human sin,
in our lives, in our nation, and in the world;
hear us, O Lord of life.

You are the Lord who does wonders:
you have declared your power among the peoples.

With you, O Lord, is the well of life:
and in your light we see light.

Hear us, O Lord of life:
heal us, and make us whole.
[*A period of silence may follow, with a concluding prayer.*]

16 O God,
the strength of the weak and the comfort of sufferers,
mercifully hear our prayers
and grant to your servant [*name*]
the help of your power,
that his/her sickness may be turned into health
and our sorrow into joy,
through Jesus Christ, our Lord. **Amen.**

Prayers for Comfort in Grief

17 Eternal God, shepherd of your people,
    we feel the fleeting passage of life,
    and we know how fragile is our existence
    on this tiny planet amid the spinning galaxies.
    We confess with the prophet:
    "All flesh is grass,
    and all its glory is like the flowers of the field.
    The grass withers and the flowers fall. . . ."
    Yet we also confess:
    "The word of our God stands forever."
    Teach us to number our days,
    that we may gain a heart of wisdom.

    We look to you as frightened children look to their mother,
    for you alone can comfort us.
    Have mercy on us, O God.
    See our tears and hear our cries
    and lead us all, as pilgrims,
    through this valley of death's shadow
    into the light of the resurrection
    of Jesus Christ, your Son, our Lord. **Amen.**
            —based on Psalm 90:12; Isaiah 40:6-8

18 Merciful God, you care for your children
    as a shepherd cares for the sheep.
    We lift up *[names]*, their parents and friends,
    for your special care today,
    for their loss is so painful
    and their grief threatens to overwhelm them.
    May they find comfort and courage in your unfailing love,
    enough trust to live without answers,
    and deep hope through Jesus Christ, our Lord. **Amen.**

19 God of compassion and love,
    you have breathed into us the breath of life
    and have given us mind and will.
    In our frailty we surrender all life to you from whom it came,
    trusting in your gracious promises,
    through Jesus Christ, our Lord. **Amen.**

20 *A prayer on the loss of a child*

> Jesus, Lamb of God,
> in your life on earth
> you welcomed children in your arms.
> And now, reigning in heaven,
> you welcome home our dear little one, [*name*].
> But our minds and hearts are numb with sorrow.
> Our pain is too great to bear.
> Surround us too with your loving embrace
> so that we will know again that we too are your children. **Amen.**

21 Man of sorrows, you truly are acquainted with grief.
> You wept at the tomb of Lazarus.
> You cried for the city of Jerusalem.
> You anguished in the garden of Gethsemane.
> You bore our pain, guilt, and abandonment on the cross.
> Thank you for knowing all our pain.
> Comfort us with the life-giving presence of your Holy Spirit.
> Give us strength to face each struggle.
> Give us peace despite our questions.
> Give us hope amid our trials.
> Give us faith in your never-ending promises. **Amen.**

22 To you, O Lord Jesus Christ, we still pray,
> even though we are stricken and terribly hurt.
> We still trust you because on Golgotha
> you did not hold yourself aloof from suffering
> but entered it and were stricken and terribly hurt. **Amen.**

Prayers of Lament

23 How long, O LORD? Will you forget me forever?
> How long will you hide your face from me?
> How long must I wrestle with my thoughts
> and every day have sorrow in my heart?
> How long will my enemy triumph over me?
> Look on me and answer, O LORD my God.
> Give light to my eyes, or I will sleep in death;
> my enemy will say, "I have overcome him,"
> and my foes will rejoice when I fall.
> **But I trust in your unfailing love;**
> **my heart rejoices in your salvation.**
> **I will sing to the LORD,**
> **for he has been good to me.**
> —Psalm 13, NIV

24 My God, my God, why have you forsaken me?
        Why are you so far from helping me, from the words
            of my groaning?
    O my God, I cry by day, but you do not answer,
        by night, but find no rest.
    Yet you are holy,
        enthroned on the praises of Israel.
    In you our ancestors trusted;
        they trusted, and you delivered them.
    To you they cried, and were saved;
        in you they trusted, and were not put to shame.

    But I am a worm, and not human,
        scorned by others, and despised by the people.
    All who see me mock me;
        they hurl insults, they shake their heads:
    "Commit your cause to the LORD; let him deliver—
        let him rescue the one in whom he delights!"
    Yet it was you who took me from the womb;
        you kept me safe on my mother's breast.
    On you I was cast from my birth,
        and since my mother bore me you have been my God.
    Do not be far from me,
        for trouble is near
        and there is no one to help.
            —from Psalm 22:1-11, NRSV

25 O LORD, the God who saves me,
        day and night I cry out before you.
    May my prayer come before you;
        turn your ear to my cry.
    For my soul is full of trouble
        and my life draws near the grave.
    I am counted among those who go down to the pit;
        I am like a man without strength.
    I am set apart with the dead,
        like the slain who lie in the grave,
    whom you remember no more,
        who are cut off from your care.
    You have put me in the lowest pit,
        in the darkest depths.
    Your wrath lies heavily upon me;
        you have overwhelmed me with all your waves.
    You have taken from me my closest friends
        and have made me repulsive to them.
    I am confined and cannot escape;
        my eyes are dim with grief.
    I call to you, O LORD, every day;
        I spread out my hands to you.

Do you show your wonders to the dead?
  Do those who are dead rise up and praise you?
Is your love declared in the grave,
  your faithfulness in Destruction?
Are your wonders known in the place of darkness,
  or your righteous deeds in the land of oblivion?
But I cry to you for help, O LORD;
  in the morning my prayer comes before you.
Why, O LORD, do you reject me
  and hide your face from me?
From my youth I have been afflicted and close to death;
  I have suffered your terrors and am in despair.
Your wrath has swept over me;
  your terrors have destroyed me.
All day long they surround me like a flood;
  they have completely engulfed me.
You have taken my companions and loved ones from me;
  the darkness is my closest friend.
    —Psalm 88, NIV

26 *The following congregational lament provides words both for general use and for particular circumstances. Use these paragraphs in any combination that is pastorally appropriate.*

[*General*]
Why, Lord, must evil seem to get its way?
We do confess our sin is deeply shameful;
but now the wicked openly are scornful—
they mock your name and laugh at our dismay.
We know your providential love holds true:
nothing can curse us endlessly with sorrow.
Transform, dear Lord, this damage into good;
show us your glory, hidden by this evil.

[*Imprisonment*]
Why, Lord, must he be sentenced, locked away?
True, he has wronged his neighbor and failed you.
Yet none of us is innocent or sinless;
only by grace we follow in your way.
We plead: Repair the brokenness we share.
Chastise no more, lest it destroy your creatures.
Hear this lament as intercessory prayer,
and speak your powerful Word to make us hopeful.

[*Illness*]
Why, Lord, must she be left to waste away?
Do you not see how painfully she suffers?
Could you not change the curse of this disaster?
Amaze us by your mighty sovereignty.
We plead: Repair the brokenness we share.

Chastise no more, lest it destroy your creatures.
Hear this lament as intercessory prayer,
and speak your powerful Word to make us hopeful.

[*Divorce*]
Why, Lord, must broken vows cut like a knife?
How can one wedded body break in pieces?
We all have failed at being pure and faithful;
only by grace we keep our solemn vows.
We plead: Repair the brokenness we share.
Chastise no more, lest it destroy your creatures.
Hear this lament as intercessory prayer,
and speak your powerful Word to make us hopeful.

[*Untimely death*]
Why, Lord, did you abruptly take him home?
Could you not wait to summon him before you?
Why must we feel the sting of death's old cruelty?
Come quickly, Lord; do not leave us alone.
We plead: Repair the brokenness we share.
Chastise no more, lest it destroy your creatures.
Hear this lament as intercessory prayer,
and speak your powerful Word to make us hopeful.

[*General*]
Why, Lord, must any child of yours be hurt?
Do all our pain and sorrow somehow please you?
You are a God so jealous for our praises—
hear this lament as prayer that fills the earth.
We plead: Repair the brokenness we share.
Chastise no more, lest it destroy your creatures.
Hear this lament as intercessory prayer,
and speak your powerful Word to make us hopeful. Amen.

27 God of life, God of comfort:
alone,
afraid,
in fear,
in loss,
we cry out:
"Why, O Lord, why?"
"How long, O Lord, how long?"
We cling to you in hope
even as we grasp for hope.
So grasp us in your loving embrace
through Jesus Christ,
who endured the cross for our sake. **Amen.**

28   O God,
whose Son knew the agony of being abandoned,
persecuted, and killed, though he had done no wrong,
hear the cries of your children who have been imprisoned unjustly.
We grieve for those who are abandoned
by their families and former friends.
While they wait for and then face their day in court,
give them hope, strength, and justice
so that they and we together can rejoice in your deliverance,
singing your praises together. **Amen.**

29   *Each section of this prayer may be followed by a sung refrain, such as "Don't Be Afraid"*
(Iona Community) or a Kyrie eleison.

O God, your people have always had their fears.
So we come to you in humility and with honesty, naming our own.
Lord, we fear the future. What is coming next?
"Will there be a place for me when I'm done
      with high school or college?" we young people ask.
"Will there be safe places for our children?" we parents ask.
"Will I die in peace and with dignity?" we seniors ask.

Lord, we fear the pain that comes
with illness and broken bones and aging.
Some of us wonder how we're going to make it
through more treatment and medication.
Some of us wonder how we can possibly face chronic illness.
Some of us wonder if prayers for healing even reach your throne.
Physical pain frightens us.

Lord, as a church, we wonder about our ministries and programs.
What if they don't "work"?
What if outreach and faith nurture don't happen?
We fear the dependence we have to have on your Spirit
to be the one to breathe life into Christians and non-Christians.

Lord, we are afraid of people who are different from us:
those more powerful than us, those poorer than us,
those of a different color or creed, those smarter than us,
those with different personalities.
How do we talk to these people, O God?
How do we make peace with them?

Lord, we have acquaintances,
friends and family members whom we deeply love
but who do not know you.
We are afraid for their salvation.

We admit, O God, that we're fearful of stillness and quiet.
It seems as if the last thing we want to do
is slow down and be attentive to you.

Help us not to shy away from quiet times,
from the simplicity of prayer, Scripture, and your presence.
It seems, O God, that, in the busyness of countless invitations
to parties and activities we are afraid to say no.

And for all those fears for which we cannot name,
we come to you, O God.
Those we cannot name because they're either unknown or unspeakable,
receive them in our silence.

We are fearful so often, O Lord,
because in our encounters with sin and evil
we find ourselves weak and poor.
We thank you so much then, Jesus,
for your actions and for your words—
for love and the promise of nearness,
which are our strength and our riches. **Amen.**

30 We are tired, Lord,
weary of the long night without rest.
We grow complaining and bitter.
We grieve for ourselves
as we grow hardened to the pain of others.
Another death leaves us unmoved.
A widow's tears fall unnoticed.
Our children know only the bitterness
already possessing their parents.
Our violent words explode into violent acts,
bringing destruction without thought or reason.
Lord, have mercy upon us.
Lead us to repentance, that we may forgive and be forgiven. **Amen.**

31 O God, resting place of pilgrims and sojourners,
so many of us are weary.
Give us rest, O God.
Our days are heavy with obligations,
and our nights disturbed by worries over them.
Give us rest, O God.
We are tired of battling old temptations and besetting sins,
tired by our defeats, and tired from despairing over them.
Give us rest, O God.
We are tired from trying to help people
who resist our help.
Give us—and them—your rest, O God.
Gracious God, Father of our Lord Jesus Christ,
who welcomed all who were weary and burdened,
inviting us to cast our cares on him,

6 Toward Expressing Prayers of, by, and for All God's People

Prayers in worship often convey powerful but unstated assumptions about the range and scope of prayer, and about the breadth and scope of God's redemption in and through the church as the body of Christ. For example, a congregation might pray often for pastors or missionaries but rare-ly for those who serve God in other ways. A congregation might pray for refugees or immigrants but not indigenous peoples, or vice versa. A congregation might pray for persons with disabilities but not pray as a group of people with a range of abilities and disabilities. A congregation might routinely draw upon biblical language about God's promises to Abraham but not pause to think about its own relationship to those promises, as Jewish or Gentile believers.

When churches discover their omissions, assumptions, or insensitivities, there is often a period of difficulties and false starts in learning to grow in awareness, mutual love, and accountabil-ity. Some attempts at responding can sound overly didactic or paternalistic. Some can sound ambigu-ous and tentative. Others may be overly specific or politicized. The context of a particular community will make a large difference in how a given phrase or approach is perceived.

The following prayers represent attempts to grow in grace and knowledge by expanding the range of people and concerns named in public prayer. A significant aim of these of prayers is simply to name groups of people and concerns that often are unnamed. Some of these prayers accomplish that by focusing on a single concern. Others list a variety of peoples and needs, leading the con-gregation to reflect on the variety of experiences, callings, and settings in which people are called to live as disciples of Jesus. These "list-like prayers" can easily be expanded by encouraging the congregation to pause and add specific petitions for each group named.

Because these prayers are shaped by local context and culture, it may be wise to discuss them among a group of discerning spiritual leaders and to adapt them to better fit local circumstances. And because this sampling of prayers can only begin the task of learning to express the prayers of the whole church, those discussions may well lead to large categories of concern not mentioned specifically here.

1   *A prayer for Jewish and Gentile Christians to pray together*

God of the promise,
as members of your body, from every tribe and nation and people,
we pray as one body—
    some of us sons and daughters of Abraham and Sarah, heirs of the promise;
    some of us Gentiles, grafted into the promises to Abraham and Sarah—
all of us fellow citizens,
members of God's household,
built on the foundation of the apostles and prophets,
with Christ Jesus himself as the cornerstone.

May your Spirit continue to build us together to become God's temple (Eph. 2:11-22)
through Jesus Christ, our Lord. **Amen.**

2   *A prayer for Jewish and Gentile Christians to pray together*

Lord God,
as you called Melchizedek to serve as "priest of God Most High" (Gen. 14:18),
as you stirred the spirit of King Cyrus of Persia (2 Chron. 36; Ezra 1),
as you caused the queen of Sheba to hear of Solomon's fame (1 Kings 10:1),
as you prompted the Roman centurion to say, "Surely this man was
    the Son of God!" (Mark 15:39),
as you called Magi from the East to worship the Christ-child (Matt. 2),
as you received the prayers and alms of Cornelius the Italian centurion (Acts 10:1-4),
as you called an Ethiopian court official to ask for baptism (Acts 8:27),
as you have called all of us, including those of us
    "who once were far away [but] have been brought near" (Eph. 2:13),
we pray that your Spirit will again be poured out on all peoples,
that people from every tribe and nation and land will rejoice at Christ's appearing.
Amen.

3   *A prayer for native and indigenous peoples, immigrants and refugees to pray together*

Triune God—Father, Son, and Holy Spirit—
we come before you as many parts of one body.
You have called us together
from different cultures, languages, customs, and histories:
some of us are indigenous peoples of the land;
some of us are refugees, migrants, or pilgrims—people on the move;
some of us are hosts; some of us are guests;
and many of us are both hosts and guests.
All of us are searching for an eternal place where we can belong.

Creator, forgive us.
The earth is yours, and everything that is in it.
But we forget . . .
In our arrogance we think we own it.
In our greed we think we can take it.
In our ignorance we worship it.
In our thoughtlessness we destroy it.
We forget that you created it
to bring praise and joy to you,
and that you gave it as a gift
for us to steward,
for us to enjoy,
for us to see more clearly your beauty and your majesty.

Jesus, save us.
We wait for your kingdom.
We long for your throne.
We hunger for your reconciliation,

for that day when people from every tribe and language
will gather around you and sing your praises.

Holy Spirit, teach us.
Help us to remember
that the body is made up of many parts.
Each one is unique, and every one is necessary.
Teach us to embrace the discomfort that comes from our diversity
and to celebrate the fact that we are unified not through our sameness
but through the blood of our Lord and Savior, Jesus Christ.

Triune God, we love you.
Your creation is beautiful.
Your salvation is merciful.
Your wisdom is beyond compare.
We pray all this in Jesus' name. **Amen.**

4   *A prayer for home life, in multiple settings and contexts*

Lord, our God,
wherever we live, we need you.
Wherever we live, you call us to serve you.
We pray for all (among us)
    who live alone,
    who live in community, as family or friends,
    who, alone or together, care for children or aging adults,
    who provide foster care,
    who live in college or university housing,
    who live on military bases or camps,
    who live in prisons,
    who live as refugees,
    who live in group homes, nursing homes, or care facilities,
    who are displaced from their homes,
    who live with conflict,
    who do not have a home . . .
        [add other petitions as appropriate]

We pray that you will provide for all of your children—
those among us and those around us—
homes of shelter and safety,
communities of loving encouragement and support,
opportunities to live as faithful disciples of Jesus, ministers of Christ's peace. **Amen.**

5   *A prayer for fruitful work and service in all sectors of society*

Lord God,
we pray for all
    who work in business and industry,
    who work in homemaking,
    who work in medicine,
    who work in education,

who work in agriculture,
who work in government,
who work in service to others,
who are beginning a new career,
who struggle in their work,
who struggle to discern your calling,
who are seeking new or different jobs,
who are retired or anticipating retirement,
who are unemployed or underemployed,
whose work is not valued or appreciated,
who are overcommitted.
Give us joy in our work, joy in using gifts and talents we receive from you.
Give us joy in doing all our work to your honor and glory.
Equip us to labor in ways that promote justice and peace.
Equip us to be ministers of your peace in a world that cries for peace,
through Jesus Christ, our Lord. **Amen.**

6   *A prayer for agents of renewal in all sectors of society*

Lord, our God,
help us to be agents of your peace in this [*town, city, township, region*].
We pray for all who work
to provide housing,
to resist racism,
to provide fruitful employment,
to provide safe schools and places of training and learning,
to develop artistic gifts,to provide health care,
to provide spiritual care,
to bear witness to your love for us in Jesus Christ,
to minister to refugees . . .
     [add other petitions as appropriate]

May we, like leaven, be your agents of peace and renew
also that all your children will flourish and glorify you.
Through Jesus Christ, our Lord, **Amen.**

7   *A prayer for prisoners, victims, and all who love them, serve them, and work with them*

God of justice and mercy,
your grace and truth shine forth through Jesus Christ, our Lord.
In a world clouded by injustice, violence, and revenge,
we pray for the strong work of your Holy Spirit.

May your Spirit bring healing, justice, encouragement, redemption, and hope
to all prisoners—
     those waiting for trial,
     those facing parole boards,
     those who are discouraged,
     those facing long imprisonment,
     those struggling with temptation,

those suffering injustice,
those recently released and trying to readjust to normal life,
those who have given up hope,
those struggling to know the difference between right and wrong . . .
[add other petitions as appropriate]

to families of prisoners—
children missing their parents,
families struggling to make ends meet,
parents who blame themselves,
those filled with fear or loneliness,
those feeling guilty,
those struggling to forgive . . .
[add other petitions as appropriate]

to victims of crime and violence, and to those who love them—
those struggling to return to normal life,
those who no longer feel safe,
those who are angry,
those who need guidance to find help,
those struggling to forgive,
those who help victims take their lives back . . .
[add other petitions as appropriate]

to all judges, lawyers, and lawmakers—
those struggling to discern wise and just courses of action,
those burdened by heavy case loads,
those overwhelmed by a sense of responsibility,
those with insights about ways of strengthening practices of restorative justice . . .
[add other petitions as appropriate]

to all who work in the prison system—
those who care for and protect prisoners,
chaplains and others who are ministers of your peace,
social workers and counselors who work with prisoners and their families,
those who feel unsafe,
those who have become apathetic or discouraged . . .
[add other petitions as appropriate]

to all communities and neighborhoods—
those who feel unsafe,
those who do not know how to welcome prisoners back,
police, security guards, and neighborhood watch groups who keep
communities safe,
those who need to learn to trust again,
those who need to forgive,
those who need to be forgiven . . .
[add other petitions as appropriate]

May your Spirit bring healing, justice,
encouragement, redemption, and hope
to your church in every neighborhood.

We pray for resolve to be ministers of Christ's peace—
>for wisdom to speak and act with truth and grace,
>for justice, peace, healing, and courage in all relationships,
>and for the elimination of prejudice and segregation.

We long for the day, Lord Jesus, when you will return
and when all things will be made new.
With urgency but also with hope we pray:
May your kingdom come. **Amen.**

8   *A prayer for all who suffer from moral injury*

God of justice and mercy,
in the middle of our war-torn world,
in the midst of moral uncertainty, confusion, and disagreement,
we humbly offer our prayers for your justice and mercy.
We pray for all peoples in every nation and culture
who participate in military activities and in the administration of justice.
Teach them—and each of us—the nature of just action and legitimate acts of defense.
We pray especially for those trained to engage in violent action—
>for those who were ordered to engage in violence that turned out not to be just,
>for those who are haunted by guilt and shame for past actions that cannot
>>be undone,
>for those who must learn to resist deeply formed habits of retribution . . .
>>*[add other concerns as appropriate]*

Through Jesus, may your justice and mercy flow to all the peoples of the world.
Lead us, as your disciples, to be ministers of your peace. In Jesus' name, **Amen.**

9   *A prayer for those affected by cognitive, emotional, relational, physical, or behavioral impairments and distress*

Loving God, we pray for all who face cognitive, emotional,
relational, physical, or behavioral impairments and distress.
We pray for those who bear pain for loved ones, themselves,
or those in their professional or congregational care.
May all draw strength, wisdom, and hope from you.
We thank you for discoveries of approaches and interventions
that alleviate suffering and promote flourishing.
Embolden us to welcome the many ways in which your care
and healing may come to and through us.
Grant us gratitude for your willingness to enter into our pain,
trust that your faithful love does not depend on our feelings,
grace and hospitality to welcome, compassion to serve faithfully,
strength to bear the weight of confidentiality,
restraint from actions and words that alienate,
wisdom to discern appropriate responses,
fervency in translating our hopes and fears into prayer,
assurance of your abiding love, and hope in your everlasting promises.
Through Jesus Christ we pray. **Amen.**

ACKNOWLEDGMENTS

Permissions

Brief portions of this book may be reproduced without special permission for one-time use only, for worship and educational purposes, in an order of service for use by a congregation, or in a special program or lesson resource, provided that no part of such reproduction is sold, directly or indirectly, and that the following acknowledgment is included: "Reprinted by permission from *Prayers of the People: Patterns and Models for Congregational Prayer*, © 2015, Faith Alive Christian Resources." This notice can appear in small print preferably on the same page on which the resource is reprinted. For all other uses, please contact the copyright holder of each resource used.

Every effort has been made to trace the owner or holder of each copyright. If any required acknowledgment has been omitted, the publisher asks that the omission be excused and agrees to make necessary corrections in subsequent printings.

Please address questions about rights and reproductions to Permissions, Faith Alive Christian Resources, 1700 28th St. SE, Grand Rapids, MI 49508; phone: (800) 333-8300; fax: (616) 224-0834; e-mail: permissions@faithaliveresources.org.

Scripture Versions and Paraphrases

Scriptural texts in this book are from a variety of Bible versions and paraphrases (used by permission and indicated below) and are referenced as exact quotations, as slight adaptations (noted as "from" a particular text), or as paraphrases or quotations coupled with additional phrasing (noted as "based on" a particular text). Abbreviations referring to the sources of scriptural texts are indicated in the left column below. An index of Scripture references (p. 85) offers additional Scripture source information as an aid to worship planning.

NIV   *Holy Bible*, New International Version. © 1973, 1978, 1984, International Bible Society. Used by permission of Zondervan Bible Publishers.

NRSV   *Holy Bible*, New Revised Standard Version. © 1989, Division of Christian Education of the National Council of the Churches of Christ in the United States of America. Used by permission. All rights reserved.

Confessions and Statements of Faith

The confessions and statements of faith used in this book are listed here in chronological order.

Heidelberg Catechism (1563), translated from the first edition of the German text. © 1988, Faith Alive Christian Resources, Grand Rapids, Mich.

Westminster Shorter Catechism, a confession of faith adopted by the Westminster Assembly of 1647. Public domain.

Our Song of Hope, approved in 1978 by the General Synod of the Reformed Church in America as a statement of the church's faith for use in its ministry of witness, teaching, and worship. © 1975, Wm. B. Eerdmans Publishing Co., Grand Rapids, Mich.

Other Sources

This list identifies some of the other sources used in this book. These sources are arranged alphabetically according to their identifying abbreviations used in the next subsection, titled Sources of Specific Texts (see p. 76).

BCP	*The Book of Common Prayer,* according to the use of the Episcopal Church in the United States of America. © 1977, Charles Mortimer Guilbert as custodian; public domain.
BCW	*Book of Common Worship* (Presbyterian Church, U.S.A.). © 1993, Westminster John Knox Press.
BCWP	*The Book of Common Worship: Provisional Services* (United Presbyterian Church, U.S.A.). © 1966, Westminster Press.
BCW-PCC	*The Book of Common Worship* (Presbyterian Church in Canada). © 1991, The Presbyterian Church in Canada.
BOS-1994	*The Book of Occasional Services 1994.* © 1995, The Church Pension Fund. All rights reserved. Used by permission of Church Publishing Inc., New York, New York.
CLCW	*The Complete Library of Christian Worship.* Volume 4, Book 2. *Music and the Arts in Christian Worship.* Edited by Robert E. Webber. Star Song Publishing Group, a division of Jubilee Communications, Inc., 1994. © 1994, Star Song; transferred to Hendrickson Publishers, Peabody, Mass. Used by permission of Robert E. Webber.
ICP	*Intercessions for the Christian People: Prayers of the People for Cycles A, B, and C of the Roman, Episcopal, and Lutheran Lectionaries.* Edited by Gail Ramshaw. © 1988, Pueblo Publishing Co., Inc.; © 1990, The Order of St. Benedict, Inc.; The Liturgical Press.
ILID	*In Life and in Death: A Pastoral Guide for Funerals.* Compiled by Leonard J. Vander Zee. © 1992, Faith Alive Christian Resources.
LP	*Leading in Prayer: A Workbook for Ministers.* Hughes Oliphant Old. © 1995, William B. Eerdmans Publishing Co.

80

OS   *Occasional Services: A Companion to the Lutheran Book of Worship.*
© 1982, administered by Augsburg Fortress. Used by permission.

PsH   *Psalter Hymnal.* © 1987, 1988, Faith Alive Christian Resources.

RCA-OW   *Reformed Church in America General Synod, Order of Worship: The Lord's Day.* © by Reformed Church Press.

RW   *Reformed Worship,* a quarterly journal. Faith Alive Christian Resources, 1986-present. Most service resources published in RW are submitted by individual churches that write their own prayers and are hereby declared to be in public domain; no further permission is required for use of these items. The only request is that *Reformed Worship* be acknowledged in any future publication. (Items from RW that are adapted or adopted from other published resources under copyright are identified by the earlier published source.)

SB-UCC   *Service Book for Use of Ministers Conducting Public Worship.* United Church Publishing House, 1969.

SLDL   *Service for the Lord's Day and Lectionary for the Christian Year.* © 1964, Westminster Press.

TWS   *The Worship Sourcebook,* (Second Edition). Calvin Institute of Christian Worship, Faith Alive Christian Resources, Baker Books, 2013. © 2013, Faith Alive Christian Resources. Individual prayers and resources prepared specifically for *The Worship Sourcebook* are hereby declared to be in public domain. The only request is that *The Worship Sourcebook* be acknowledged in any future publication (see note under Permissions, p. 79).

WAGP   *With All God's People: The New Ecumenical Prayer Cycle.* Compiled by John Carden. © 1989, WCC Publications, World Council of Churches.

WAS-1   *Worship for All Seasons.* Volume 1. *Selections from* Gathering *for Advent, Christmas, Epiphany.* Edited by Thomas Harding. United Church Publishing House, 1993.

WAS-3   *Worship for All Seasons.* Volume 3. *Selections from* Gathering *for Pentecost, Summer, Autumn.* Edited by Thomas Harding. United Church Publishing House, 1994.

WBK   *The Worshipbook—Services.* Prepared by the Joint Committee on Worship for Cumberland Presbyterian Church, Presbyterian Church in the United States, the United Presbyterian Church in the U.S.A. © 1970, Westminster Press.

WN-II   *Worship Now—Book II: A Collection of Services and Prayers for Public Worship.* Compiled by Duncan B. Forrester, et al. © 1989, Saint Andrew Press.

WNYHL   *We Need You Here, Lord: Prayers from the City.* Andrew W. Blackwood, Jr. Baker Books, a division of Baker Book House Company. © 1969, Andrew W. Blackwood, Jr.

WWB   *A Wee Worship Book.* Wild Goose Worship Group. GIA Publications, Inc., 1999, fourth incarnation. © 1999, Wild Goose Resource Group.

Sources of Specific Texts

The following table lists sources of specific texts used in this book, arranged by item number and including abbreviations of original sources (such as BCW, BCP, TWS, and so on) as identified in the preceding subsection, Other Sources (pp. 80-81).

Abbreviations Used in This Table	
alt.	altered
attrib.	attributed to
c.	circa (around)
p., pp.	page, pages
PD	public domain

For example, to find the source information for resource number 5 in section 1 (Invitations to Prayer), see resource 1.5 below.

Various standard abbreviations are also included in this table and are identified in the box above.

Resource	Incipit	Source
1.1	(We offer now . . .)	TWS
1.2	(We join our . . .)	TWS
1.3	(We pray together . . .)	TWS
1.4	(We offer our . . .)	TWS
1.5	(Let us join . . .)	TWS
1.6	(Let us bring . . .)	TWS
1.7	(Let us pray . . .)	TWS
1.8	(God calls us . . .)	excerpt from "Invitations to Prayer" in WAS-3, p. 64. Reprinted with permission.
1.16	(The prayer our . . .)	TWS
1.17	(God is the one . . .)	excerpt from "Invitations to Prayer" in WAS-3, p. 64. Adapted with permission.
1.18	(Nothing in all creation . . .)	TWS
3.9	(Lord, in your . . .)	PD
3.10	(Let us pray . . .)	PD
3.11	(Gracious God, hear . . .)	PD
3.12	(For your love and . . .)	PD
3.13	(God of grace . . .)	PD
3.14	(Heavenly Father . . .)	PD
3.15	(O God, hear . . .)	PD
3.16	(Holy Spirit, our . . .)	PD
3.17	(Holy Spirit, act . . .)	PD
3.18	(Healing Spirit . . .)	PD
3.22	(In the strong name . . .)	TWS
3.23	(In the name of . . .)	PD
3.26	(To your holy name . . .)	PD
3.27	(Loving God, we . . .)	TWS
3.28	(Ever-faithful God, . . .)	BCW-PCC, p. 33, alt.
3.29	(Almighty God, Father . . .)	BCP, pp. 101, 125, PD
3.30	(Almighty God, you . . .)	attrib. St. John Chrysostom (c. 347-407), PD
3.31	(Gracious God . . .)	TWS
4.1	(Address to God . . .)	TWS
4.2	(We praise you. . .)	TWS; last paragraph from BCW

4.3	(We praise and . . .)	RCA-OW, alt.
4.4	(Sovereign God, King . . .)	TWS
4.5	(O Lord and Father . . .)	LP, pp. 194-195, alt.
4.6	(Almighty God . . .)	Andrew B. Doig in WN-II, p. 51 [39], alt.
4.7	(O great God . . .)	TWS, by Scott Hoezee, pastor of Calvin Christian Reformed Church, Grand Rapids, Michigan
4.8	(O God, whom . . .)	TWS, by Scott Hoezee, pastor of Calvin Christian Reformed Church, Grand Rapids, Michigan
4.9	(Lord of creation . . .)	TWS, by Scott Hoezee, pastor of Calvin Christian Reformed Church, Grand Rapids, Michigan
4.12	(Our Father in . . .)	TWS
4.13	(Lord, our Lord . . .)	TWS
4.14	(O Lord, we . . .)	TWS
4.15	(No matter where . . .)	TWS
4.16	(Praise the Lord! . . .)	TWS
4.17	(Lord Jesus, you . . .)	Edith Bajema in CLCW, vol. 4, bk. 2, pp. 810-811, alt.
4.18	(Gracious God, we . . .)	Louise Mangan in WAS-1, p. 43. Reprinted with permission.
4.19	(Let us bring . . .)	Harold M. Daniels in BCW, p. 111 [94], alt., PD
4.20	(In peace, let us . . .)	from Eastern liturgies of St. Basil and St. John Chrysostom (4th cent.), PD
4.21	(Lord God, because . . .)	WWB, pp. 16-17
4.22	(Let us pray for . . .)	BCP, pp. 388-389, 394 [3], alt., PD
4.23	(Bound together in . . .)	ICP, p. 30, alt.
4.24	(Almighty God, in . . .)	SLDL, pp. 17-19; WBK, pp. 31-33; BCWP, p. 33, PD
4.25	(Lord, draw near . . .)	WWB, pp. 61-62, alt.
4.26	(Eternal God, whom . . .)	WWB, pp. 77-79, alt.
4.27	(In the brief . . .)	TWS
4.28	(Loving God: We . . .)	TWS
4.29	(Lord God, thank you . . .)	TWS
4.30	(Loving God, thank . . .)	TWS
5.1	(Lover of all . . .)	SB-UCC, p. 288 [403]. Adapted with permission.
5.2	(Creator God, convenience . . .)	TWS
5.3	(How crooked is . . .)	TWS
5.5	(Father, we give . . .)	WNYHL, p. 43
5.6	(Almighty God, you . . .)	RW 43:41
5.7	(We pray to you . . .)	from a prayer for use on Rogation Sunday, Evangelical Church of the River Plate, Argentina; from "Confessing Our Faith Around the World IV: South America" (p. 10), 1985 World Council of Churches Publications, Geneva
5.8	(From many places . . .)	TWS
5.9	(Let us pray . . .)	adapted from part of a prayer in WWB, p. 105
5.10	(Most merciful God . . .)	Ministry with Persons with AIDS, Ministry with Persons with Life-Threatening Illness, and Ministry with Persons in Coma or Unable to Communicate, © 1992, United Methodist Publishing House. Used by permission.

5.11	(Lord Jesus Christ . . .)	Ministry with Persons with AIDS, Ministry with Persons with Life-Threatening Illness, and Ministry with Persons in Coma or Unable to Communicate, © 1992, United Methodist Publishing House. Used by permission.
5.12	(Eternal God, you . . .)	Ministry with Persons with AIDS, Ministry with Persons with Life-Threatening Illness, and Ministry with Persons in Coma or Unable to Communicate, © 1992, United Methodist Publishing House. Used by permission.
5.13	(O Christ, our . . .)	adapted from part of a prayer in WWB, p. 105
5.14	(Almighty and . . .)	*A Service of Healing I* and *A Service of Healing II*, © 1992, United Methodist Publishing House. Used by permission.
5.15	(God the Father . . .)	BOS-1994, pp. 167-168, adapted
5.16	(O God, the strength . . .)	BCP, p. 458, alt., PD
5.17	(Eternal God, shepherd . . .)	ILID, p. 90
5.18	(Merciful God, you . . .)	TWS
5.19	(God of compassion . . .)	OS, p. 106, alt.
5.20	(Jesus, Lamb of God . . .)	TWS
5.21	(Man of Sorrows . . .)	TWS
5.22	(To you, O . . .)	TWS
5.26	(Why, Lord, must . . .)	Calvin Seerveld in PsH 576, © 1986, Calvin Seerveld
5.27	(God of life . . .)	TWS
5.28	(O God, whose . . .)	TWS
5.29	(O God, your . . .)	RW 56:36
5.30	(We are tired, Lord . . .)	T.A. Patterson, Presbyterian pastor (N. Ireland) in WAGP, p. 79, alt.
5.31	(O God, resting . . .)	TWS
6.1	(God of the promise . . .)	TWS
6.2	(Lord God, as you . . .)	TWS
6.3	(Triune God—Father . . .)	TWS
6.4	(Lord, Our God . . .)	TWS
6.5	(Lord God, we . . .)	TWS
6.6	(Lord, our God . . .)	TWS
6.7	(God of justice . . .)	TWS
6.8	(God of justice . . .)	TWS
6.9	(Loving God, we . . .)	TWS

SCRIPTURE REFERENCES